T0278115

GREATNESS

IS A

CHOICE

GREATNESS
IS A
CHOICE

ETHAN PENNER

Foreword by Julius "Dr. J" Erving

WILEY

Library of Congress Cataloging-in-Publication Data is Available:

ISBN 9781394185757 (Cloth)
ISBN 9781394186198 (ePub)
ISBN 9781394186204 (ePDF)

Cover Design: Wiley
Author Photo: Courtesy of Author

SKY10055093_091123

I dedicate Greatness Is a Choice *to. . .*
My Granny, Mary Damsky and to Maria "Kiki" Garay,
who both taught me love and devotion.
My five children, Daniel, Rebecca, Julianna,
Michael Angel, and Everest Gobena. I hope that I've
been a good dad to you and that you enjoy the
amazing journey of life that lies ahead.
And to Marisol, a pillar of strength and love.

CONTENTS

PART TWO: FINDING YOUR GREATNESS
IN THE WORLD

PART THREE: THE FOUNDATIONS OF A
GREAT SOCIETY

★ ★ ★

FOREWORD

Greatness is a complicated topic. It is a concept that can be very confusing given its various meanings, and whose pursuit can often send one down a very unfulfilling path. I was very fortunate to grow up with my mother's great guidance. The deep sense of service and foundational religious values that she instilled in me have always helped me find my true north as a human being even when flying very high and nearly touching the sun. I have been blessed with much, but these gifts from Mom have been among my most valuable treasures as I have navigated the complex life that I've been given.

Another great gift has been the numerous outstanding people I have met along the way who have taught me, guided me, and supported me in moments of grief and darkness. Ethan Penner is high on that list of people, and I am honored to have been asked to write this foreword for his book. I met Ethan on a basketball court – well sort of. I can definitely tell you that, despite his physical limitations, he is a true competitor who brings his all to everything he does, even a semi-ridiculous game of one-on-one with a much taller, much more athletic NBA legend (me). I've known Ethan for nearly three decades and have rarely met someone who balances his impassioned love for and commitment to his family and his friends with his business pursuits and his spiritual explorations as well as he. Ethan is a man who truly walks the walk in every facet of his life and is clearly very well equipped to offer his reflections on life's true meanings, as he has done so beautifully and generously here in this book.

I doubt that any thinking person will read this book and agree 100% with everything, but knowing Ethan as I do, that is not the point. He is not a person to try to persuade others to his way but instead someone who shares his perspectives humbly and generously, knowing that others will naturally have their own to share back with him. He is a learner and a grower at the highest level. I love Ethan as a brother and love this book as his great expression to the world of his observations and lessons learned during a life of incredible accomplishment that he has lived with an unparalleled spirit of generosity and love for others.

I know that you will all enjoy this book as I have.

With gratitude,
Julius "Dr. J" Erving

PROLOGUE
GREATNESS IS A CHOICE

Some people will ask you to believe that greatness is a gift bestowed only upon a fortunate few. That is a lie, and you shouldn't buy into it. One of the most important life lessons I've learned is that greatness is not a gift but an actual choice we can make throughout every single day. Of course, nobody can be truly great at everything, but we can aim for greatness in every little thing we do, with the outcome being that we'll be great people, great friends, great parents, great partners, great lovers, and great in our careers.

I am a great man. I don't say this because other people think I'm great, although it is nice to hear this once in a while and especially from those closest to me. I don't say this for any external reasons related to status nor due to any gifts I was blessed with from birth that I had no hand in creating. I've arrived at this opinion of myself because I aim to bring my very best to every moment and to every encounter and relationship in my personal and professional life. I am focused on achieving the most from each blessed moment – the most joy, the most fulfillment, and the best outcome in every way. I consciously try to bring maximum value to all people I come across and make the most of the minutes of life I've been blessed with. When I lie down every night, I am peaceful knowing this about myself, and when I awaken to begin my new day, I am emboldened by it. I wrote *Greatness Is a Choice* because I know that greatness is available to everyone, but each person needs to believe in that and see a path to greatness for themselves. The feeling of self-worth I enjoy is the most valuable thing I possess. It brings me immense joy and is the foundation of a fulfilling life. I want this book to help you find the unique path to experience those same feelings as you discover your individual greatness.

I've been fortunate to be exposed to greatness up close many times in my life, beginning with the great effort of my single mother to raise me and my brother. Those experiences have helped me understand the nature of greatness, and by sharing those thoughts and experiences with you, I hope you'll unlock many ideas that will fortify the choices you must make in your own life.

One of my most memorable experiences took place in 1994 when I hosted a weekend retreat for about 500 real estate industry luminaries and their spouses. Our gathering at the Boca Raton Resort in Florida culminated with a Saturday night dinner and concert in the hotel's ballroom. That concert was a surprise performance by the legendary Sir Elton John, and the story of this encounter is one that I hope will be as eye-opening and inspiring for you as it was for me.

As dinner was being served, Elton's longtime agent Howard Rose invited me backstage to meet Elton, where he was waiting to go on stage. When I entered, and as the introductions were made, I noticed Elton was visibly nervous. He had achieved legendary status long ago, so I was quite surprised by his demeanor. I asked him if he was okay, and Elton admitted that he was on edge for this particular performance. He told me that when he played large venues, he knew everyone who came to the show was a fan because they bought tickets and purposely chose to see him. But here, in the Boca ballroom, he was uneasy because the people at this retreat were invited guests to a surprise concert, not even knowing who the performer would be. He expressed concern to me that maybe they'd not like his music.

Stunned by this extreme expression of self-doubt from such a legend, I assured him that he'd be fine and everyone would love his performance. I don't specifically recall everything else I said, but I remember saying, "Don't worry. You'll be fine. You're Elton John."

That night, he stepped on stage at the Boca Raton Resort ballroom with no accompaniment other than his piano, and he gave one of the single greatest musical performances that I or anyone there will ever witness. Elton played nonstop for two and a half hours, singing every hit in his catalog and leaving the audience stunned and forever marked by their up-close experience with such greatness. I was not more than 25 feet from the piano and was blown away by his magic. After the show, Howard Rose told me it was at the very top of hundreds of shows he had seen Elton perform since the beginning of his career. The man, the experience, and the lesson I learned from observing how he manufactured the mental state to achieve greatness will stay with me forever.

Elton was born Reggie Dwight, a young man with some musical skills for sure but no special advantages over other talented young musicians. What made him Elton John was his passion for greatness, his belief in himself, and his willingness to give it his 100%. That experience contrasts many choices I've seen other talented people make, squandering and often not even noticing opportunities for greatness. People like Elton can clearly inspire us, but we cannot copy anyone and find true greatness. For that, we must perfect ourselves. With this book, I hope to inspire you to a higher level of awareness and discover your unique life's purpose and value.

You will also note, and hopefully appreciate, the brevity of *Greatness Is a Choice*. I once heard Mick Jagger say that great art leaves unanswered questions and room for personal interpretation, and I am surely aiming for "great" here. As someone who has embraced religion and spirituality, I think of Mick's teaching as akin to leaving space for God to talk to us or through us. I hope this book can accomplish that. I have resisted the temptation to write a longer book filled with more personal stories that might hammer home these ideas. Instead, I invite you to fill in the gaps for yourself, examining your life for stories that can bring personal meaning to these ideas. Life's journey is highly personal, and no two people experience it the same way. *Greatness Is a Choice* contains lessons and ideas borne from my journey, and I'm offering them to you with the hope that you can interpret and use them in the unique context of your own life.

PART ONE

THE GREATNESS IN YOU

CHAPTER 1

YOU MUST ADMIRE YOURSELF

When you wake up and look in the mirror to shave or wash your face, it's imperative that you admire the person that you see in the mirror. If you do, your day is bound to be just fine, regardless of the challenges you face. If you don't, then nothing else matters, and there's a good chance that your day will be miserable.

When we're kind, generous, and honest to others or give our fullest and best effort toward a goal, the real payoff is that we gain legitimate admiration for ourselves.

Too many people lack genuine self-esteem, which is the only esteem that really matters. Instead, these people invest great efforts toward gaining the approval of others. I see a world filled with lost souls that I attribute largely to this wrongheaded pursuit of external esteem. We can see this playing out in our personal relationships, business dealings, and how we project ourselves into the world, including the car that we drive and the home that we live in, and especially in online media, where "likes" and "thumbs-up" emojis are the most highly prized form of currency.

People who chase the approval of others often act in deplorable and self-destructive ways as part of an endless pursuit of material gains and emotional payoffs. These pursuits and the compromises people make to find bigger paydays and a false sense of an inflated version of who they are, completely undermine the one thing that really matters - self-esteem.

We must stop chasing what we think would be impressive to other people and instead be the person who embodies the qualities that we know in our hearts are truly admirable. We may be able to fool others and gain their esteem, but we know the truth about ourselves, and only this truthful self-evaluation, or self-esteem, matters.

Greatness and self-esteem are intrinsically linked. There can be no fulfillment or true comfort and joy until you have earned the admiration of the only judge that matters – you.

CHAPTER 2

WHAT IS YOUR LIFE'S PURPOSE?

People can be divided into two groups: those who see a world as having been built with intelligent design, and thus see their own lives as purposeful and a part of that design, and those who see a random world and, therefore, struggle to find purpose. Few people ask themselves the critical question that I was fortunate enough to have been indoctrinated with by my parents: What is my life's purpose? However, it wasn't until I began a daily prayer ritual that included prayers that alerted me to the amazing, intelligent design of the world and of our bodies that I began to understand and feel the true power of purpose.

In a random world with no purpose, there is no assurance of justice. That view of the world is a frightening one, and when people are filled with fear, the rule of the jungle is natural reaction. That we see a world with so much violence, misery, depression, poverty, and confusion clearly shows how many people live according to a belief in a random world.

Yet, with just a little awareness and inquisitiveness, it is not hard to see that the world has been created with serious intelligent design, meaning that there must be purpose. The workings of our bodies are a great example. When our digestive system functions properly, we consume foods, gain energy, and eliminate the remains. Yet, we rarely stop to appreciate the miracle of that system, usually not until it breaks down. I experienced this kind of physical breakdown a few years ago, and it forever changed how I think about my bodily functions and my appreciation for their intricate perfection. Observing nature is another excellent way to gain awareness of the world's intelligent design. I love sitting outside on my porch, staring at trees, listening to birds chirping, smelling flowers, sipping a glass of scotch, appreciating the miracle of the moment, and how blessed I am to be a part of that amazing landscape. I get the same feeling when I hike, jump in an ocean or lake, or watch a sunrise or sunset.

Seeing the world as one that has been intelligently designed is a logical precursor to seeing our lives as having meaning and purpose. With this, we naturally respect ourselves, our bodies, the planet, and others, all of which empowers us to live lives of contribution and purpose. That, in turn, leads to a sense of fulfillment.

An understanding of purpose also helps us constructively deal with pain and disappointment. In those moments when things don't go our way, many of us who see randomness will blame bad luck or others. One who sees intelligent design and, thus, purpose, will be more likely to take responsibility and ponder the lessons taught by the experience, knowing that, however disappointing or painful, it was meant to be.

That is the definition of believing in a purposeful world that produces learning and growth. Armed with this belief, we can live with less fear, knowing that the inevitable tough challenges are purposeful, valuable, and part of a grand plan.

CHAPTER 3

PRAYER IS POWERFUL

A few years ago, I had a "born again" moment at the bar mitzvah services of the son of a dear friend. As I read the prayers in the prayer book for the first time, the words and meanings made sense to me. It felt as though God was speaking to me in a personal manner. To say that I was moved would be an understatement. I returned home and recounted the experience to my wife, Marisol, who suggested that I should continue praying daily, which she had been suggesting for many years. Suggestions I had largely ignored.

Although I grew up with religion and was familiar with the Hebrew prayers, I had never paid attention to their meaning. I also never cared for the idea of reciting words that were not mine. The thought seemed completely wrong and disingenuous. Until that day, I believed that my relationship with God was mine and that the words should also be mine. Inspired by the bar mitzvah experience, I gave in and began to pray from the Hebrew prayer book daily. In the years since, I have found continual beauty and brilliance in it. Over time, though I recite the exact words daily, my awareness and understanding grow continuously. This routine has changed me, and I honestly could not have written this book without it.

I have come to realize when praying, that I am not praying *to* God per se but that by reciting the prayers each morning, I am reminding myself of the many things I must do to make the coming day the best day possible. Each day my prayers remind me of the blessings I have awakened to, including my health, my family, my financial capability to live a decent life, and even the miracle of having good ideas pop into my head. My prayers reinforce an awareness that the world is indeed purposeful and was created in a manner that functions in amazing ways. From these daily insights, I gain appropriate personal humility, knowing how weak and fragile I am. That realization invariably enables me to let myself off the hook when I fail despite my greatest efforts, knowing that I'm a small part of a much bigger plan.

My prayers let me see the world as purposeful and perfect rather than random, and this helps to bring me great comfort when things don't happen according to my plans and dreams. In those moments, I understand that my plans perhaps weren't the best and that a better fate awaits me than the one I had in mind. The triumvirate of awareness of intelligent design, purposeful living, and a prayer ritual delivers those ideas that create a foundation for living a great and meaningful life.

CHAPTER 4

BE HUMAN

The daily competition for resources to provide for ourselves and our families defines most of our waking hours. Some are better at this game than others and produce more, but for everyone the competition and the associated pressure to provide comes at the price of deadening our souls and challenging our ability to be human.

Our desire to meet our needs can naturally pit us against our fellow men and women, which places us at odds with the Golden Rule of treating others as we wish to be treated. Somehow humans must find a way to balance the need to produce and provide with our spiritual need to be good and caring, and in harmony with all other beings and creations.

I believe that the best response to this challenge lies in prayer and in finding a higher degree of divine connectivity. One prayer in particular has served me well in this regard. It is a portion of "The Amidah Prayer," a daily Jewish prayer that praises God as the reviver of the dead. In fact, it is this prayer that helped me to fully appreciate this daily challenge that we face. It goes like this:

> Sustainer of the living with kindliness, Resurrector of the dead with great mercy, Supporter of the fallen, and Healer of the sick, and Releaser of the imprisoned, and Fulfiller of His faithfulness to those who sleep

in the dust. Who is like You, Master of mighty deeds, and who can be compared to You? King Who causes death and restores life, and causes deliverance to sprout forth.

For most of my life I thought this was a ridiculous prayer and a relic of ancient ignorance. I saw it as rooted in some belief in a ghoulish revival of dead bodies, maybe like a bad Halloween horror film. But I was reading it too literally and interpreting it only in a physical context. Then one day a completely different meaning dawned on me, and since that time this prayer has become vital for me.

Every morning as I recite it, I realize that there is a higher calling than the daily battles we face and that only by connecting ourselves spiritually can we discover and manifest our true humanity. Being human for me begins with connecting to my creator and then to all other beings and creations in a benevolent and harmonious way. It sets me up to enter my business day insisting upon "win–win" outcomes rather than the "I win–you lose" outcomes that too many seek.

In this gentler state, I become a more unique and authentic version of the person that I aspire to be. These qualities frame how I compete by aligning my worldly needs with my spiritual values. Imbued with this state of awareness, I can bring my humanity, uniqueness, and authenticity to all parts of my daily life.

If you do not pray regularly, there are probably other paths to becoming more human. You must find those that are meaningful and important to you. One way might be to challenge yourself to live by a moral code and to remind yourself of that code regularly. Embracing a life filled with compassion, integrity, respect, discipline, humility, a sense of justice, freedom from prejudice, and many other traits are choices you get to make.

With or without prayer, you choose greatness when you bind yourself to principles that align with the highest and most noble paths to create more humanity in your life.

CHAPTER 5

RISK IS LIFE

Risk is at life's core. It sounds terrible, something to avoid, yet risk is inherent in all facets of life, and avoiding it is tantamount to avoiding living. If we never love, we can never have our hearts broken. If we never share and trust, we can never be betrayed. If we never have children, we can never feel the unimaginable pain of a child's suffering. If we never chase our dreams, we can never have our dreams shattered. Of course, if we never do these things, we've chosen not to live. Very little happiness or success is available in any part of life without taking on risk.

My life has been a mix of successes and failures, but mostly it has been defined by my commitment to striving, trying things, and the willingness to fall, fail, learn, and grow.

I'm not too big on famous quotes, but one that I read in my youth is attributed to the German philosopher Goethe: "Be bold and good things will follow." This ethos has always been at the forefront of my life. Many people are daunted by life's challenges, seemingly frozen into indecision and inaction. This quote has always inspired me as a call to action and to accept that I may not get things right at first. But I will have the opportunity to learn, grow, and improve along the way.

I definitely didn't start out knowing what it took to build a good family, as my parents were poor role models. I think I've gotten pretty good at it after 40 years, two marriages, and parenting five kids. Along the way, I know I screwed up often, caused my fair share of pain, and experienced plenty of it myself. But the journey was rich and filled with great joys. I wouldn't trade the overall experience for an easier, less involved, or less chaotic one.

In other parts of my personal life and work, I have also charged forward, trying things and always being open and vulnerable. This approach has resulted in a high degree of career success with many warm and meaningful friendships and relationships. However, I've also experienced the deep pains of betrayal that vulnerability can naturally produce. The price was always worth the rewards, and hopefully, with each price paid, I became smarter and stronger.

Trying means sometimes failing, if not often. Thankfully, trying also means succeeding sometimes, too. But if we fail in a state of awareness and personal responsibility, it means learning, growing, and improving. I'm here on this earth to live, to test myself, to learn, and to grow . . . and so are you. Sign me up for trying and for failing, too.

Taking risks also often means letting go of the safety net of the status quo to have the best chance of getting the things you want. That may mean walking away from a business deal instead of accepting terms that are unfair or walking away from an unfulfilling relationship like a job or a marriage. To find excellence and what is right for you, you must have the courage to walk away, often without a safety net. Of course, this seems risky. I would argue though that you lose more by staying put in something that is not working for you. When you're willing to walk away from a suboptimal situation, you send a clear message to others about how important an issue is to you. That usually gives you the best chance of getting what you want. The other party will work to accommodate you and improve the situation, or you'll be out of that relationship. Both outcomes represent huge upgrades.

So, in many cases, the perception of risk is just an illusion. There is little real downside. You will either get what you need in that relationship or will be liberated from a futile situation and free to find your path to fulfillment. The key is maintaining a commitment to following through with cutting ties unless there is change on the other side. If you're not truly committed and you make threats but don't follow through, all your leverage is stripped away and your future efforts will be seen as bluffs that won't be taken seriously. The definition of risk in these situations means that you can't be entirely sure of outcomes. Sometimes you'll get what you want; other times, you won't. Be prepared to accept that you often find yourself out in the cold, searching for new relationships or deals.

The payoff for taking measured risks is well worth any potential negative consequences, which will be temporary as long as you keep looking for what you want and never give up.

CHAPTER 6

THE SPECTER OF DEATH

Nothing is more certain than the fact that every physical human life ends in death, and none of us knows for sure what happens next, if anything. I think this specter of death looms large in guiding our daily lives and not necessarily in the healthiest ways.

For most people, the idea of our mortality plants a deep sense of fear that distorts much of our thoughts and actions. That fear creates a craving for security, which is largely unavailable in this world. In our zeal to find it, we often set aside all common sense and easily fall prey to any promise of security. History has repeatedly shown that people will trade away their freedom, follow orders, strive to control others, and do terrible things to their fellow humans for the illusion of security. Wars are typically fought in the name of security.

I've dealt with the fear of death constructively through several realizations. First, I am keenly aware that I am not my body. My actual, conscious being controls my physical being. And by using that distinction, I become aware that there is an Ethan Penner and an Ethan Penner's body, and they are not the same. When I want my finger to move, I will it to do so. The moving finger is not me. It is Ethan Penner, or the real me, who is commanding the finger to move. From this, I can glean that my body will decay and die, but that part of me who controls my body – the energy and force that cannot be seen or touched and whose literal existence is thus doubted by most – will not die.

Next, I understand that just as my birth is unexplainable – where did I come from, and why am I here? – so is my death. Birth and death are simply the bookends of the natural cycle of the physical human life. In fact, our lives have meaning and purpose *because* an end is looming. Without that end, there would be no urgency and no purpose. Imagine a game that had no end. There would be no winner and no reason to bring any effort. The score at any point during the contest would be meaningless. Endings in all that we do are necessary for the journey to have meaning and purpose.

Each of us must reckon with fear and insecurity in our effort to make our lives joyous. Succumbing to our desire to find security in an inherently insecure world is a recipe for chaos and disaster.

CHAPTER 7

TIME IS EVERYTHING

Time is precious. People don't appear to appreciate this enough and waste a ton of it, our most valuable resource, recklessly on things that don't matter. Equally egregious is how we allow others to waste our time. And we waste massive amounts of time with the wrong people. We spend too much of it with those with whom we have no real connection rather than with people we treasure, can learn from, and grow with.

It mortifies me to see how people do not prize their time enough or the time of others, acting as if there is an endless supply. So much time is spent on nonsense, arguing about things that don't matter, or engaging in the ugly practice of gossip. As we get older, many (but not all) of us gain a greater appreciation of how valuable and finite time is.

I believe pursuing greatness is fundamentally linked to deciding how to best allocate time. I also believe that kindness and thoughtfulness are concepts that are rooted in the respect for the time of others, and I thus view brevity as a sign of deep consideration for others. I've frequently been asked to speak at industry gatherings and conferences and have always felt obligated to deliver real value to those in the audience who have invested their precious time to listen to me. I've also sat in the audience at many such events and have been frequently disappointed at how willingly speakers will eat up the audience's time and give them nothing of value.

With the many social media options for information and entertainment readily available in our pockets, it wouldn't be too big a stretch to suggest that today's generation may be the most egregious time wasters of all history.

One of my pet peeves has been the significant increase in road traffic. As recently as 20 years ago this was only a big-city problem, and not too long before that wasn't much of a problem anywhere. In the past decade, since about 2010, it has become a global issue in towns and cities, big and small. The combination of corrupt and incompetent leadership and no proper planning has led to people regularly sitting in traffic for hours at a time. That is literally highway robbery. If you spend two hours a day sitting in traffic and your typical waking day is 16 hours long, you've lost 12.5% of your productive time for no good reason. At this rate, over 20 years, you've wasted two and a half full years of your life sitting in your car in traffic. The fact that this has not become a major political issue is a sign of people's high level of complacency and low awareness, which may be as disheartening as the reality of the lost time.

Finally, I've observed that we often only exist alongside people but are not really living with them. We are so busy, wrapped up in our lives, and distracted by our phones, that we are not there even when we are physically right there. Even with those special people, our time is often hurried or superficial. As I grow older, I find more than ever that I crave time well spent with people I love and care about and whose company I find so valuable.

CHAPTER 8

THE GROUND BECKONS

The ground beckons,
Resolute and firm.
It is non-negotiable,
With its partner, the worm.
Man strives to elude it,
Hurtling ships into space.
Man strives to defy it,
With athleticism and grace.
Place your ear to it,
And listen to its hum.
Pay careful attention to it,
Heed its wisdom.
The ground has been there,
Seen that, heard it.
The ground has encountered all,
And devoured it.
The ground seems silent,
Even peaceful and calm.
The ground is an actor,
It is a monster with charm.

CHAPTER 9

SACRIFICE IS A PREREQUISITE FOR GREATNESS

If you were to ask people if they want to be successful, as I have done annually in my opening class that I teach at graduate business school, you'd likely find that virtually everyone answers with a resounding "Yes!" Yet, I'm consistently amazed at how few people understand that you must focus and sacrifice if you want to accomplish anything in life.

When you want to build muscle, you must sacrifice your physical comfort and exchange it for pain in the gym. If you want to be a great spouse or friend, you must compromise and invest in someone else's interests. To have career success, you must sacrifice parts of your personal and social life and put in the extra hours.

Lots of people talk a good game. But the odd disconnect is that only a small percentage of those people are willing to do what it takes to succeed. Thinking and wishing about something is much different from committing to a worthy goal and doing whatever it takes to reach it. Ultimately, one's true goals can be judged solely by actions and never words.

If you can't grasp the simple concept that sacrifice is a prerequisite for greatness, you should stop reading this book now and pass it along to someone who does.

CHAPTER 10

WE MUST HONOR OUR BODY

The deterioration of personal health in society during the course of my lifetime has been astounding. Despite a proliferation of health-related businesses and services, and massive education efforts to heighten awareness, poor health remains a growing problem.

It seems like you can't go a block in most American cities today without passing by all kinds of health and exercise offerings. We've been inundated with traditional gyms, yoga and Pilates studios, and spinning studios, martial arts dojos, and dozens of other formal exercise options. There are also countless online and brick-and-mortar vitamin and health food stores, wellness regimens, weight loss programs, diet and holistic fads, and more exotic alternatives like hyperbaric chambers and cryotherapy studios. Entire sections of bookstores and libraries now devote considerable shelf space to health and wellness topics in what has become a multi-billion-dollar industry.

In my parents' time, gyms were rare and mostly the exclusive domain for men. Few people exercised in a formal setting, and for the most part, nobody even went out for a jog or a run. Almost nobody "exercised" in a traditional sense. There was no concept of healthy food or nutritional education, and the knowledge of exercise physiology was quite nascent. And yet, the generations before us had far lower rates of obesity and related diseases than we see today.

Today, despite all of the businesses aimed at health and fitness, our society has lost its way when it comes to taking proper care of our bodies. It's stunning how little we care for the vessel that we count on to carry us through life's journey. There can be no question that general unhealthy living, too much stress, too little sleep, the burgeoning use of technology, highly questionable food quality, and heightened levels of alcohol and drug use have all added to today's tragic state of affairs.

If you are fit, you may ask why you should care about this trend. Why is the physical well-being of others any concern to you? Part of the answer lies in the fact that we live in a society where the costs of many bad decisions are socialized. The consequences of these bad decisions are borne by both the individual who chose them and society at large. Contrary to the popular belief that America doesn't have socialized medicine, in reality, we do. No emergency room can reject someone because they can't pay. And when insurance companies set the price of insurance premiums, they must account for the overall health, or lack thereof, of the broad segment of people whom they insure. So, even if you make healthy choices that result in lower incidences of illness, you'll still pay more for insurance than you would otherwise in order to cover the expected higher healthcare costs for those in our society who make poor lifestyle choices.

For example, during the COVID-19 pandemic, data clearly indicated early on that those who were obese and had other comorbidities were at far greater risk for bad outcomes than those who were not. Although other factors were in play, it's also not too far of a stretch to suggest that to some degree the severe impositions that were placed on the broader society, including masking, keeping kids out of school, shuttering businesses and houses of worship, no weddings, no funerals, or large gatherings of any kind, were implemented to protect a smaller segment of our society, many of whom had made bad lifestyle choices.

On a societal level, the burden of poor health choices is massive and unsustainable. It's also selfish and unfair. On a personal level, it saddens me to see that individuals who can make changes that will lead to longer and healthier lives refuse to do so at alarming rates.

CHAPTER 11

YOU HAVE THE POTENTIAL FOR MAGIC

The world seems to naturally gravitate toward a state of chaos and disorder. There is a human quality, however, that runs counter to this, and that is the magic of being productive and constructive. This productive force is all too rare, and when we see it show up in abundance in certain people we are appropriately amazed, awed, inspired, and even envious. Steve Jobs, Tina Turner, Mother Teresa, and John Lennon all had it. Great athletes like Michael Jordan had it. This magic energy is the personal foundation that enables us to bring love into the world, warmth and affection, caring and support, hope, optimism, and inspiration. It is something that we all have but that we need to dig deep to bring out. Religion teaches that we are all made in God's image; maybe this is what I'm referring to.

This innate greatness that we all possess is often inhibited by doubt and insecurity, fear of failure, and laziness, all of which turn us into negative, critical, and pessimistic forces. If you can find a way to bring out the magic from inside of you, then you're special. You are among those whom the world will rely on disproportionately for its advancements, inspiration, and comforts.

In my business life, I've always strived to fill unmet needs, reasoning that if I do this, I'm producing real value and will be rewarded. This is perhaps the highest form of productivity as it involves taking on challenges deemed too daunting a task for anyone else to have ever taken on. If you can help meet unmet needs in your life journey, I am confident that you will be richly rewarded in every way possible, and deservedly so.

CHAPTER 12

LIFE IS HARD FOR A REASON

Tests help to push us to our higher potential and to gain real self-esteem, which is why they must be challenging with a real prospect of failure. If they're not, then meeting and passing them has little value.

During my lifetime, there has been a 180-degree shift on this topic. In my childhood, we learned that there were winners and losers through the games that we played. We also learned that life could be painful and painfully unfair, and that by being challenged we could learn how to bounce back from those tough moments when they inevitably arise in the future. I still remember crying my eyes out many times as a kid after suffering disappointment or physical injury. My mom would always tell me in a comforting tone that life could be harsh and unfair at times and to try and learn from my experiences.

But somewhere along the way, as my generation became parents, we decided that it was a good idea to deprive our children of all pain and the lessons born from being tested and failing. We gave out participation trophies to everyone rather than honoring winners. In doing so, we inadvertently taught our children so many wrong lessons, the biggest of which was to deprive them of resilience and thus undermine their preparation to compete and thrive in the real, challenging, and competitive world.

The resulting political correctness that we see today, where sensitivity to people's feelings trumps honesty, starkly contrasts to the mantra taught to my generation, "Sticks and stones may break my bones, but words can never hurt me." For youth today, life's challenges are still there in all their glory and, in some ways, more complex than ever. But many young adults are forced to get "on-the-job" experience trying to handle these challenges on the fly with pitifully poor preparation. That means they will likely suffer greater failures and pains as they navigate the tests of life.

These tests of life are part and parcel of human existence on earth. They are here for a reason, and we must embrace and grow to meet them. My friend and teacher Paul Chek is fond of using the term *pain teacher*, which fully captures the role of pain in our lives. Rather than hate our pain or quickly mask it with chemical agents and forget about it, we ought to embrace it thoughtfully as our best teacher. When we experience physical or emotional pain, we should scrutinize things and ask ourselves, "What message is this pain trying to communicate, and what changes should I make to learn from this experience?"

In my experience with pain, which has been quite severe at times, I've found that if I can take a deep breath and view it as a benevolent teacher rather than a dreaded enemy, I can learn and benefit even in the worst circumstances. And, very interestingly, when I take this approach and even welcome the pain teacher, it actually hurts much less.

CHAPTER 13

WORK IS NOT
A FOUR-LETTER WORD

Too many people have had a poor understanding of or hostility toward the concept of work. Most people see work as a necessity for survival and not as a potential source of joy and fulfillment well beyond the financial rewards that it might bring us. One of the most valuable lessons I learned is that service for the benefit of others through your work is key to turning something that has long felt like drudgery into the prime source of genuine happiness and personal fulfillment.

Several years ago, I attended a seminar hosted by Tony Robbins. One of the exercises involved writing down what we did for a living. I dutifully scribbled that I made real estate investments on behalf of my investors. Tony then asked us if we thought our writing was inspiring to ourselves or anyone else. Of course, I did not. You could tell by looking around the room at that moment that no one at the seminar did. He let us off the hook when he explained that no job is fulfilling when viewed through the lens of the specific actions that we take. Even the most glamorous jobs often boil down to a function that is quite boring. Take an actor's job as an example. Stripped away of the glamour, it requires reciting memorized lines in front of a camera. Defined that way, it sounds like anything but fun or exciting, which I can attest to since I've done some on-camera work.

Tony then asked us to rethink our response and instead to write down what we did in our jobs that benefited others. I wrote that by making sound investments, I protected people's hard-earned money from loss and provided them with income to help them pay for things like their kid's college education or retirement. As I reviewed what I wrote, my spirit soared with pride that I had never felt about my career. Until then, despite having immense success, my work was not a great source of personal pride because I only thought of my work as a means of providing for my family. At that moment, I started to understand that when I did my job well, it provided huge value to so many others. I realized that a life of purpose where we use our skills to help others is the key to living a life of joy and fulfillment. And the opportunity to bring value to others is something that is available at every single job. Work is the place where we get to bring ourselves to the world, to share our spirit, to test ourselves and our ideas, and to come away with a beautiful combination of fulfillment and learning. Work is the centerpiece of our lives and is where we can best act out our purpose.

CHAPTER 14

PERSONAL RESPONSIBILITY

When we don't properly care for ourselves or handle our business we unwittingly burden others. Given that life is hard for everyone, and everyone has their challenges to attend to and their hopes and dreams to pursue, asking others to bear this additional burden is grossly unfair. On the flipside, someone who attends to a high standard of personal responsibility and handles challenges with cheer is to be greatly admired.

When my kids have either neglected to take care of their schoolwork or attempted to lean on me too heavily, I have pointed out to them that I have my responsibilities, which include my job, which happens to support their lifestyles. I've taught them from early ages that they need to handle their own business with the same level of commitment that they see me handling mine. My goal here has been to teach my children the value of being strong and independent, and to respect the limited time that others have to handle their responsibilities.

The same idea about personal responsibility can also be applied to our state of mind. When we show up somewhere, maybe at our jobs or the dinner table, dejected or angry, we are abdicating our responsibility and imposing our challenges, or their effects on others. That is not right. We owe it to others to handle our business with grace, and when we do show up in their lives to be of added value rather than be a burden.

I remember an extreme example when my daughter Julianna threw a little tantrum during her terrible-twos stage just as we sat down for our family dinner. I took her aside and calmly explained to her that she had every right to scream and yell, but she did not have the right to ruin the family's tranquil dinner. I told her that she could go to her room, close the door and continue her tantrum there, and when she was done, she'd be welcome to rejoin the family. To my amazement, she did exactly that, and I learned a valuable lesson in parenting that day.

Consistent with this commitment to personal responsibility in our conduct, we must also remember that happiness is a choice. We cannot fully control what occurs in our lives, but we can control how we react. One of the simplest truths that seems not so well appreciated is that happy people make the world a better place, and unhappy people make it worse. We can and should always choose happiness.

CHAPTER 15

THE STEEP PRICE OF DISHONESTY

Dishonesty is theft. When we're given wrong information or have the right information intentionally withheld from us, we will make bad decisions that lead to poor outcomes. The result will be that we will have wasted our time ... our most precious and rare resource.

Dishonesty takes many forms, sometimes even those that start out as having been well-intended. But even these seemingly benign examples are sure to be harmful. For example, when someone wrongly compliments us, we risk investing more time into an arena that is not likely to be very rewarding. Therefore, I've always been super-honest with my kids, taking great care not to give them misleading feedback. Instead, I recognized that, as one of their greatest influences, I have an obligation to let them know when they're doing well and when they're not. The negative feedback can be tough to hear, but I'd rather be honest than mislead and hurt them even more later on. As a result, I have earned standing with my kids. They always know that they can trust my integrity, which is so valuable in any relationship. Of course, I carry that same mindset into all of my personal and business relationships.

Today, we live in a time of extreme political correctness where purposely providing false information to support a specific agenda or not to hurt someone's feelings is not only okay but is actually the preferred way of doing things for many. One of the biggest lies in recent times that illustrates the massive societal costs of political correctness involves obesity. Anyone paying any attention since the new millennium has witnessed a global surge in obesity rates and, along with that, surging rates of serious illnesses related to being overweight. When the scourge of COVID-19 hit, those who were obese suffered much worse fates than the rest. In my opinion, one of the contributing factors to all of this is that our society has made it unacceptable to be honest and risk offending certain groups of people. Thousands, if not millions of people paid a horrible price as a result.

The desire to not offend has been extended to published medical standards that identify the level a person would be considered to be overweight and the level considered obese. Those standards have adjusted to the point where they are now laughably off base and of little value other than to support flawed talking points. That continued dishonesty means many will continue to be complacent because their doctor tells them that they fall into an acceptable category. These fake "pass" signals being given to spare hurting feelings will have the disastrous effect of perpetuating bad habits and poor health when alarm bells should be ringing loudly instead. Ultimately, the idiotic policy of institutionalized dishonesty has led to a surge in health costs that is an unnecessary burden on our society, and it has also destroyed the lives of many who may have responded differently if the messaging had been more honest.

Honesty is often a difficult and risky choice. Being honest can absolutely hurt others' feelings and even put a relationship at risk. In the end, honesty is also the most generous gift that we can give to another because it is so valuable and often so hard to give. If you always choose honesty, your life may have some conflict, but in the end you will sleep much better at night.

CHAPTER 16

THE BUBBLE OF JOY

We all know how to have fun when we're young. But as we get older and life's responsibilities grab our attention, we seem to lose touch with fun. I have noticed for a long time now that although people don't have as much fun when they get older, the craving for it never subsides. One of my secrets to success in all facets of my life has been to make sure that there is fun around me at all times.

It wouldn't be a stretch to say that this adult fun deprivation is a meaningful contributor to the high level of unhappiness and dissatisfaction with life that seems pervasive. As I entered adulthood and the working world, I noticed how rare fun and smiles were for most people. I saw that competition undermined camaraderie, and drudgery squashed creativity. I also noticed that older, more experienced people seemed to have really given up on the idea of fun, and they were quite content to share their miserable demeanor, seemingly without really even being aware. They were digging themselves into a deeper hole of unhappiness and spreading it far and wide. They had become messengers of negativity.

It was about at age 27 when I was recruited to a senior job at Morgan Stanley, and I was surrounded by too many such dour people, that I experienced an epiphany. I realized that if I created a fun work environment around me, or what I call a bubble of joy, I would distinguish myself. I figured, who wouldn't want to work inside that bubble of joy, and what customer wouldn't want to transact within it? I even called the group of mostly young and energetic men and women who gravitated to work with me then "The Can-Do Club," and we enjoyed each other's camaraderie both in and out of the office. As my Wall Street career grew, I leaned on this insight heavily and it has never failed me.

When I finally got to be the head of my own business, I had a beer refrigerator installed in my office, and at 5 p.m. there was free beer for all. As a result, it was common for much of my company and even our close clients to be seen hanging out together well into the evening, sharing beers, socializing, and doing business in a joyful setting. Often this led to groups of us going out to dinner, karaoke bars, and clubs afterwards. But the real fun high-water marks back then were the many parties that I hosted for both company outings and client events, with the highest level of musical entertainment. I became quite famous for these, and an invitation was the real estate and finance industry's hottest ticket in the 1990s. I know that so much of my career success, and certainly the value of my personal brand, is attributed to my deep commitment to joy. My reputation for being a terrific guy to work for and with has always helped me to attract high-quality people as well as a steady stream of business opportunities.

I have two close friends who have implemented the bubble of joy philosophy in their professional lives better than anyone I know. Mark Morse and his family founded The Villages, an unbelievable community in Florida for what they call "active retirees." The Villages is just fun all day and night, seven days a week. Mike Meldman founded Discovery Land in the 1990s and has developed private residential and resort communities around the world that are bubbles of joy for those families privileged enough to visit or live in them. Mark and his family and Mike saw an unmet demand for joy, filled it beautifully, and have been handsomely rewarded with success and fulfillment.

This commitment to living inside of a bubble of joy doesn't stop at work. If you care about your life and the others whom you meet or have a relationship with, you will find ways to have fun and share it. Embracing this mindset is a tremendous recipe for success in life. My friends Jim "Watty" Watson and his wife Kimmy have embodied this ethos in their daily lives better than anyone that I know. Regardless of life's challenges, they are always smiling and generously spreading their beautiful positive energy. When you create a bubble of joy around you, your life and those lucky enough to know you will be greatly enhanced. You will be a magnet, attracting the best, brightest, and most aware people who demand that their days be joyous. And this will result in you living in greatness and in joy, just as the Wattys do.

CHAPTER 17

DON'T SHARE YOUR UNRESEARCHED OPINIONS, PLEASE

We are frequently asked for our opinions or are offered opinions from others. What do you think of this person, or this situation? This seemingly harmless chitchat or gossip is actually quite harmful. An all-too-common refrain these days is that everyone is entitled to an opinion. This implies that everyone's opinion is essentially valid. Yet, unresearched opinions that are based on hearsay have no validity whatsoever. Articulating, mindlessly quoting, or forwarding them on social media gives them weight and is therefore dangerous. This sharing does nothing other than perpetuate ignorance and untruths. It is important to understand that words are powerful and must be measured carefully.

Of course, it is perfectly fine, even admirable, to not have an opinion, to simply say nothing or "I don't know." This silence is an attractive sign of humility and intelligence. Those who know very little often have strong opinions about many things and are delighted to share them. At the same time, those who know something are very aware of the limits of their knowledge and are generally much more cautious to share their thoughts. In fact, those in this latter group are more likely to be the ones asking questions rather than providing answers.

Talking more and slinging opinions around recklessly is not appealing on any level and doesn't bring any form of greatness to the world. We can all benefit by being more cautious before speaking and more economical with our words.

CHAPTER 18

FULFILLING POTENTIAL IS FULFILLING

One of the most important but vexing lessons that my dad taught me is that there is no greater sin than unfulfilled potential. He frequently lectured me with those exact words over the years. I was always puzzled about what exactly it was that he meant by the word *potential*.

Once I found my way into my career, which was quite by chance, as I knew no one in the field of finance and had no real prior awareness or understanding of it, I began to achieve success. As the typical rebellious son, I continually tried to disprove my dad's teaching by trying to run away from my skills and potential, not wanting to be a slave to them. Instead, I was focused on pursuing what I thought was "true happiness." Despite a steady path of success in finance and real estate, I always wondered if my true destiny may lie elsewhere. I was reluctant to give in and enjoy the fact that I had found a career path where I began to achieve my fullest potential.

Over the years I've gained an appreciation of the deep wisdom of my father's mantra and have come to acknowledge that he may have been right. I've observed that we are born with innate gifts and skills, and by cultivating them to their highest levels and applying them to maximize their benefit to the world, we can experience genuine ful-fillment. I found that success and achievement are very fulfilling.

That is one of the attractive qualities of free market capitalism. It gives us freedom and guides us to create opportunities that provide society with maximum value. As the famous economist Adam Smith observed long ago, capitalism provides an invisible hand that steers us to where we are at our best. Following the path on which this hand guides us gives us the best chance of fulfilling the highest version of our potential. This leads us to enjoy the benefits of our successes and the pure joy and self-esteem that come from making a meaningful contribution to our society.

Think about this hypothetical example that I like to use in busi-ness school when considering the benefits of capitalism. Let's say a boy dreams of being a baker and owning a bakery one day. However, try as he may, he has no aptitude for baking, and his baked products taste terrible. In a communist society, if he's a relative or family friend of a local politician, he may be granted the town's sole bakery license because of his connections. Thus, the townspeople would be doomed to eat terrible baked goods, and the poor baker would be roundly dis-liked and have no sense of personal fulfillment. Without free-market capitalism, this young man would be deprived of the harsh but proper feedback that he is a horrible baker, which, had he received it, would have forced him to redirect his efforts elsewhere to more productive endeavors.

In a free-market capitalist society, the inept baker who receives that powerful negative feedback would either learn his craft better or go bankrupt and close his bakery. The upside would be that he would be spared a lot of wasted time from a wrongheaded pursuit. Instead, armed with lessons learned from his free-market failure, the ex-baker would be compelled to seek out and then develop his true talents and skills, and be better positioned to make a meaningful contribution to the lives of others. I guarantee he would lead a happier life, and society would be much better off.

When you pay attention to your skills and talents and create opportunities to keep refining them and putting them to the best possible use, you have also chosen to create a framework to fulfill your potential. That lesson is universal regardless of your profession.

CHAPTER 19

THERE IS NO DISCIPLINE, ONLY FAITH

The concept of discipline is false. I believe that there is no such thing as people with more discipline than others. Instead, those who seem to have more discipline are those who have more faith in positive outcomes. They can imagine a better version of themselves and are willing to invest in that vision.

My wife, Marisol, is amazing in many ways. It's no exaggeration to say she has been among the fittest people on Earth. She possesses an incredible ability to dedicate herself in the most disciplined way. Indeed, she prides herself on her discipline. She will do whatever it takes to get the outcomes she wants and readily admit that sacrifice, structure, and consistency all play a primary role in those efforts.

Before meeting her, I had long struggled with being chubby despite my reasonably high level of athleticism and lifelong commitment to working out. Under her tutelage, my body transformed. I will never forget one day, after training with her for months, looking in the mirror in a washroom and barely recognizing myself. At that moment, I understood the fallacy of the concept of discipline. I realized that we all walk around with a picture of ourselves embedded in our subconscious, and this picture is our greatest limiting factor. It defines us and thus limits us, robbing us of our ability to dream of being better. For years, I walked around with a picture of myself as a chubby guy, not a lean one, and this vision robbed me of the ability to change. This limiting vision of myself related to my physical state, but I am sure that the vision we have of ourselves, and that anchors us, stretches well beyond the physical to encompass all facets of life. Some of us see ourselves as being dumb, or boring, or poor. These visions undermine our chances to grow, change, and achieve.

Changing a body from fat to one that is lean and muscular requires intense dedication to a long journey of sacrifice. It requires giving up many things that we consider to be joyous, including tasty foods and relaxation, and replacing them with real pain and discomfort. As I have explained to Marisol, many people would only make those sacrifices if they could believe there would be a payoff and that they'd have a physique like hers. However, it would be completely illogical for anyone to make these sacrifices if they doubted that the outcome would be good, and thus worth the sacrifices. With that picture of our chubby selves embedded inside of us, it should be no surprise that we quit when things get tough in our journey toward improvement. We decide that because we'll never be better than the embedded picture of ourselves, it makes no sense to make the sacrifices.

The more I thought about it, the more I realized that people everywhere have these same thoughts when confronted with hard challenges. When faced with the sacrifices and investments that we must make to have a chance at any positive change, we naturally, and mostly subconsciously, ask ourselves if we believe that we can truly change and, thus if the effort to even try is worth it. Too often, most conclude that it is not, which prevents people from having what we have come to label as "discipline." Taking it to absolute terms, I believe that there is no discipline. There is only faith. An attempt at improving by finding discipline will always fail until we establish unwavering faith in our ability to achieve a better outcome. That is true whether we're trying to transform our bodies or any other aspect of ourselves or our lives.

Imagine how hard it is for young people growing up in impoverished neighborhoods to bring it hard in school where no story of any past success can be found. There is no history to create a framework of faith, which is why it is so hard to break out of endless cycles of underachievement. For too many, there is no vision for a better tomorrow, which will continue to undermine any well-intended efforts to bring about positive change. Before we can ask anyone to work hard to achieve a better future, that person must first be able to imagine and believe in a greater version of himself. Getting to this mental state is no small feat. It is the most common barrier to achievement and one that we must all master to achieve growth.

CHAPTER 20

QI

Qi is a Chinese concept described as a universal life force that flows in all organic life forms. Its existence and properties are the basis of a good part of Chinese philosophy and medicine that balances a person's spiritual, emotional, mental, and physical health.

We all have Qi (pronounced "chee"), but few fully understand how to harness and deploy it to our greatest advantage. When our Qi operates optimally, we are happier, healthier, more productive, and more capable of "bringing it hard" in all areas of our life.

I learned about Qi years ago when I took kung fu lessons in New York from a master monk who taught me how to summon my Qi when punching. When he punched, he moved into a different state of consciousness to fully harness his Qi. His eyes rolled to the back of his head, and he would let out a scream whose origins were from the depths of his soul. I learned to mirror him and will never forget the feeling of force I could generate. It was exhilarating. For a time, I looked at everything, everywhere, and wondered, "Can I punch through this?" My family got a kick out of this as I contemplated putting my fist through our home's exterior wall and even through our dining room marble table, which was about 6 to 8 inches of solid marble. The power I felt inside me made me feel like I could take on anything.

All of us have this massive life force, and I believe we must learn to tap into it to achieve any form of greatness, but the proliferation of technology has made this more difficult in recent years. Our quest for comfort has made our lives easier, but it has also given way to a higher degree of laziness, which has, in my observation, become debilitating and has distanced us from our own powerful Qi.

These tech advancements have replaced much of active living with tools such as our incredibly powerful portable phone, virtual reality, hundreds of television channels and programming on demand, and video games, and have facilitated everything being easily delivered to our doorstep in short order. When I was younger, people had to hop up from their sofas just to change channels on their television. Today, many people don't have to leave their sofas at all, and unfortunately, many have grown accustomed to that way of being.

Greatness comes from channeling your full and powerful energy into active and worthy pursuits. I fear that too many people have lost that connection with their Qi, and in the process, have seriously compromised their lives. There is a simple fix for this. Discipline yourself to stay away from technology for blocks of time. Get off the sofa. Go outside, walk, and get in touch with nature. Engage in physical fitness activities and maybe even take some kung fu lessons. To activate your Qi, find something you enjoy that gets you moving, and do it regularly. The surge of power that you will discover within yourself will be thrilling.

CHAPTER 21

MUSIC IS ETERNAL

Music has always been an integral part of my life. I'm sure that's the case for almost everyone because it is one of the few universal things in the world that not only binds us to each other but also plays a powerful role in regulating our state of mind. It is interesting to note how music created decades or even centuries ago can still bring significant joy to our lives. History forgets most people, but music lives forever.

Music first affected me when I was three and my mom bought the earliest Beatles albums and played them for me repeatedly. To this day, I know every song and the order that they appear on those albums. In my youth, I grew to love the original metal rock sound, especially Black Sabbath, whose gritty sound and "us against the world" sentiment resonated with my blue-collar upbringing. I learned how music could affect our state of mind when I'd loudly play Sabbath, Deep Purple, or Jimi Hendrix to amp myself up for basketball games. Later I discovered and fell in love with the raw energy of Twisted Sister. Seeing them live in clubs in my teens imbued me with powerful energy that propels me decades later when I play their music. I used music to pump me up well into my Wall Street career. In my 20s, I played U2's

Under a Blood Red Sky album on a loop every morning for over a year from when I woke up until the moment that I burst onto the Morgan Stanley fixed-income trading floor, ready to conquer the world.

As I moved along in my career, my passion for music intersected with my business life in a way that was quite unusual for a finance, investment, and real estate man, and was a literal dream come true for me. In the early 1990s, I saw that the world of real estate was desperate for financing, and I created a path for the bond investor to fund real estate, for which I gained some degree of fame. To make this happen, I had to build a bridge of trust between real estate owners and institutional bond buyers, two groups of people whose paths had never before crossed. I chose to use music as my tool.

Before that time, the notion of bringing in musical greats for private corporate events was quite rare. But I noticed that the Wall Street legend of the 1980's Michael Milken had done this successfully at exclusive annual weekend retreats to build a bridge between lesser-known entrepreneurs needing capital and the same bond buyers whom I hoped to introduce to fund real estate. Mike's retreats were called *The Predator's Ball*, and our retreats at Nomura were known as *The Showcase*. The Showcase name was part of a strategy we used as a tribute to our elevated commitment to the music. During a five-year run, including our annual Showcases and other events that we hosted, more than 100 of the most legendary musical acts ever known performed for us. That list included Elton John; the Eagles; the Allman Brothers; Crosby, Stills & Nash; Bob Dylan; Stevie Wonder; Sting; Stevie Nicks; Roger McGuinn; and Chicago, to name a few.

When the *Wall Street Journal* wrote a major article about our company and me, I was given the moniker *the Rock' n' Roll Banker*. The truth is that every person who shared those magical musical experiences with me and each other remains forever bonded. I have made major contributions to finance and real estate, but I sometimes think that by using music in my business life as I did and sharing these amazing experiences, my brand in the industry was truly built. Music is that powerful.

Music is highly personal, and you should never have to apologize or defend the type of music you choose to enjoy. We all have different musical preferences based on our memories and internal rhythm – that largely unexplained "something" that uniquely resides in each of us. Many people have tried explaining why music affects us so, but in some ways, I hope that mystery is never fully unraveled. There is a magic that comes from feeling the joy, energy, sadness, and a full range of emotions that only music can elicit, without fully understanding why. That is a big part of what gives music its eternal qualities.

Another part of the magic of music is sharing what you like with others. With that in mind, let me share some recommendations that continue to bring me great joy today. U2's "The Fly" remains special to me because there is a moving guitar solo about halfway into the song. I close my eyes, turn the volume up, and I'm moved to tears. To this day, the Beatles' love songs also touch me. My personal favorites include "And I Love Her," "Here Comes the Sun," and "In My Life." And, of course, I still listen to Black Sabbath regularly, usually with a small and satisfying grin on my face, and always in the gym. Music can help us find our "true north" by bringing us back to our essence and reminding us of who we are at our core.

CHAPTER 22

FINDING PEACE AND JOY IN NATURE

Growing up I didn't think of myself as too much of a nature person. Yet, even in my mostly paved neighborhood in Yonkers, New York, my friends and I found wooded areas, played in the dirt, and were fascinated with creatures like worms and summertime fireflies. Today, it seems that technology has displaced children's playfulness in general and the love and appreciation of Nature in many.

I know that I had become disconnected from Nature as an adult until I met my wife, Marisol, who literally climbs trees for fun. Thanks to her, I rediscovered the importance of appreciating and treasuring Nature and noticing its beauty, power, and perfection. Now, one of my favorite pastimes is to sit outside and gaze at the trees, listen to the birds, and breathe in the life-affirming scents of Nature. My appreciation of Nature has helped me to see God and purpose in a world that can often seem to be random and thus frightening.

In our fast-paced world, we are all busier and more stressed than ever, and in response, many of us use artificial means such as drugs and alcohol to calm ourselves, dull our pain, and make our world slow down. Those choices are less than optimal, especially when the best medicine, Nature, is all around us and costs nothing. The adage of stopping to smell the roses has never been more essential than in these times. I encourage you to do that regularly so that you can find the peace and joy we all need more than ever.

PART TWO

FINDING YOUR GREATNESS IN THE WORLD

CHAPTER 23

CHOOSING WHOM TO SHARE YOUR LIFE WITH

When deciding whom to choose as a life partner, a business partner, or even a friend, it is common to make a list of qualities that we prize. Lists will often include things like intelligence, sense of humor, kindness, or maybe good looks. What I've learned is that, although these lists are important as are the qualities, they are a distant second in importance, because they focus on the other person rather than on yourself. In my opinion, the most important criteria when choosing with whom to share your life is the impact that person has on you. If the person inspires you to be your best and to produce the fullest version of yourself, then that is a special person who should be treasured. If the person has an opposite impact on you, then regardless of their other fine qualities they really have no business in your life. It really is that simple.

CHAPTER 24

THE DEBILITATING EFFECTS OF THE VICTIM MENTALITY

At age eight I was given my first bike as a gift. It was a green banana seat bike with brakes built into the pedals rather than on the handlebars, so to stop you had to push backwards on the pedals. After about a week of riding it endlessly first in the playground and then on the street, I finally built up enough courage to take it down a big hill. As I mounted the bike atop the hill, I was really nervous, and as I threw my leg over the bike and jumped on, my worst fears were quickly realized. I hadn't gotten my leg sufficiently over the seat, so my foot was not on the pedals as gravity took over and me and my bike began picking up speed down the hill. Somehow, I ended up airborne, flying through the handlebars, landing on my knees and sliding down the hill on rocks and broken glass, with my bike ultimately catching up to me and hitting me in the back and head. It was humiliating and painful, and now I found myself a quarter of a mile from my apartment with blood pouring down my legs. I had no choice but to gather myself and walk my bike home, steeling myself against the pain and just handling it.

When I entered my apartment my grandmother and mother were there and on seeing me they both shrieked in horror at the site of my bloody legs. Instantly, my resolve dissolved into self-pity and fear, and I burst into tears. I know that I was only eight, but at that moment I learned how debilitating a victim mentality can be. It can turn us from strong to weak. Since that moment, I have learned to not show sympathy for anyone, regardless of how painful or harsh their circumstances may be. I have empathy, which means that I understand when people are struggling or suffering, and in those moments, I genuinely wish for them that they can find the strength and resolve to overcome their challenges. However, I will not show sympathy for them, knowing that doing so will only harm them by robbing them of their strength and resolve, thus undermining their natural ability to meet their challenges and overcome them.

Today's culture seems to be one in which the victim mentality has been broadly embraced, and even celebrated. I believe that this will lead to more people being less capable of meeting challenges and, as a result, fewer people who will even be bold enough to seek out challenging paths. That is surely not a healthy thing for our collective future.

CHAPTER 25

DUALITY

Duality may be the most complex observation that I've come across, and it is also my personal favorite. This concept, which is the notion that two contrasting things can coexist and both be true is naturally puzzling and uncomfortable to accept because we are often taught differently. And yet, duality seems to be ever-present.

For example, it is hard to argue against the idea that a single life is meaningless and that nothing a person does will likely be remembered or have a lasting impact. If we buy into this, we can conclude that we shouldn't take wins or losses too seriously. That perspective has real value in getting us through tough times. Yet, at the same time, our life is all that we have, and it thus follows that each minute is precious and must be treasured, honored, and lived to its fullest potential. Without this perspective, it is hard to imagine anyone ever accomplishing anything or finding any joy. Although these two ideas seem to contrast directly, I believe they must somehow be embraced simultaneously in some sort of a strange balancing act.

Another example of duality is how we strive for a balanced life that includes seeking joy in each minute while making sacrifices in the present for a better future. Which is it? Both, right?

And then there is the eternal debate as to which societal construct is superior. Is it one that controls humans very tightly, fearing their worst inclinations? Or is it one that provides great freedoms, honoring that each life is precious and unique and must be left to express itself while on its journey? Who among us has not found themselves on both sides of this debate?

In embracing duality, it is tempting to conclude that there is no black and white, only gray. But even that cannot be true, and the opposite of that must be considered and accepted. For if there is truly no black and white, then there are no truths, and without truths, one cannot live. There are truths, which are black and white, yet there are also many, many contradictions in life, each with kernels of truth that flicker like the stars in the sky from bright to dark. That is the essence of duality, which seems to be the essence of life on earth.

We can gain wisdom and balance by contemplating opposing and seemingly contradictory perspectives and, in the process, become far more empathetic to others. This alone would do wonders to provide us with more productive lives freer of friction. Appreciating and embracing duality will naturally lead us to be less judgmental toward those who act or believe differently than ourselves, and instead encourage us to learn and understand different perspectives than our own.

Duality is an enlightened approach that can feel complex at first, but the more you wrestle with this coexistence of seeming opposites, the more you will learn and gain wisdom you can apply to your life.

CHAPTER 26

HONOR YOUR ANCESTORS AND YOUR LEGACY

I was born to Jewish parents who had many family members perish in the Holocaust and whose entire generation was scarred by it. Their parents fled a hostile situation in Europe and were blessed to gain entry to the United States in the 1920s and 1930s. However, they came with no useful work or language skills, or connections to help them find their footing in this new and strange land. When I reflect on my grandparents' lives, they seem to have been an ongoing struggle for survival. Unlike so many today who whine that they're not having fun or are not being properly respected, my grandparents and their generation never expected fun, good times, or any accommodations to their needs and sensitivities. Their world was hard, and they fought mightily to put food on the table for their families.

At the same time, I remember my grandparents as eternally giving and almost always focused on their grandchildren. It was obvious that they knew that their legacy would be tied to how well their descendants' lives turned out. My four grandparents, and especially my maternal grandmother, taught me the value of giving selflessly to others. My granny was a true saint. More than anyone I've known, she showed devotion to me and my brother's needs, the memory of which inspires me daily. Inspired by her, I try to lead a life of generosity, imbued with an abundance mentality.

Although my grandparents came to America without a formal education, they understood that education was essential to achievement and steered their children in that direction. My mom and dad both achieved extraordinary academic success. My dad graduated college at 17, and my mom was a Phi Beta Kappa at Barnard College at Columbia University. Although high, this level of academic achievement was not unique among their generation of Jews born to European immigrants.

In addition to a heightened academic focus, the care for each other was integral in bolstering the post-Holocaust Jewish community in the United States and throughout the globe. This love and caring for others and welcoming them into your home are qualities rooted in biblical Jewish teaching going back to the story of Abraham welcoming the three strangers who were wandering in the desert. That historical orientation toward communal support was heightened during the Jewish diaspora when Jews were strangers in European lands and often the victims of hostility. It eventually culminated with the shared tragedy and existential crisis of the Holocaust in the 20th century.

This community bond remains strong today for Jews around the world. Having traveled extensively, I've always known that I could enter a Jewish house of prayer anywhere and would be taken in warmly by that community. To this day, I do not doubt that I would be offered food and lodging and be connected to the local Jewish community, who would step up and assist in any way they could. It is a part of my heritage that I have embraced personally, always opening my home to friends, family, and strangers from all backgrounds. It has made my life and the lives of my family much richer. Of course, this cultural hospitality and communal nature are not unique to the Jewish culture, as I've encountered similar welcoming in other cultural communities. I mention it here in appreciation for my heritage.

The Holocaust's lessons were unique as they were born from truly extreme circumstances. My grandparents and their generation witnessed ordinary and otherwise decent people, many of whom were neighbors and even friends, turn on them and even murder them just because of their Jewish faith. I am certain that this led to a communal survivalist instinct that became a life-affirming inspiration and a part of my heritage. I believe it helps explain the levels of post-Holocaust success that Jews have had in business, politics, science, the arts, and all other fields. I also know that suffering and hardship are a part of the story for all United States immigrants and indeed for most family histories, and that the stories associated with them can, and sometimes do serve as inspiration for later generations just as my ancestral stories do for me. Unfortunately, it seems that for the most part, these stories of sacrifice are not passed down as often or as prominently as they should be today. In the Jewish community and beyond, I am disappointed that my children's generation has largely lost their connection to their inspirational history. Today, I see too many young people of all backgrounds, spoiled and complacent, unwitting beneficiaries of their ancestors' blood, sweat, tears, and sacrifices. I write this as a call to arms for everyone to learn and retell the stories of their ancestors' hard work, risk-taking, and sacrifice so that our descendants can forever live in a state of gratitude rather than entitlement.

The lessons of becoming rooted in my heritage were not solely a Jewish thing nor tied to the Holocaust. I learned to be proud of my heritage for many reasons and from many different influences. Although I grew up in a poor area of Yonkers, New York, our mailing address showed us living in the more affluent neighboring town of Bronxville. It was common for many people, including me, to hang onto this thread of status and claim that we lived in a better neighborhood than we did as a way to feel better about ourselves. That changed for me after a grizzled older man who coached one of my Little League teams told us in no uncertain terms to be proud to say that we were from Yonkers. He got me thinking a lot about many things that day, not least of which was to be unconcerned with status or the opinions that others have of you. It just doesn't matter at all. From then on, I've been unabashedly proud to tell people that I'm from Yonkers, with all that implies.

To this day, I live with a continual appreciation of having grown up in a neighborhood surrounded by people who endured the struggles of having just enough to scrape by. I will forever have deep respect for the grit and resilience displayed daily by those living in areas like Yonkers, and many even more challenging neighborhoods, who have no choice but to bring it hard daily even though the odds are stacked against them. The experiences and challenges we faced as a community in Yonkers shaped me then and continue to define me to this day. My roots emanate from where I was born and raised, including the Bronx, where I spent my first seven years, and the teachings and customs that I was exposed to from my grandparents, parents, and relatives.

Rituals are also a great way to pass along heritage. With many holidays tied to historical and biblical stories, this is something that the Jewish community does quite well. To this day, my family perpetuates the tradition of welcoming the Sabbath each Friday evening just as my father and mother did and as their ancestors did before them. Each Friday before dinner, I sing songs over the wine and bread, bless my children, and praise my wife just as my ancestors have done for thousands of years. This Sabbath tradition alone has deeply strengthened our family's bond while providing me an ongoing opportunity to connect my children with their ancestors and their sacrifices. It has been an excellent time to remember and share my heritage with my family.

Honoring your ancestors and heritage and passing that along to children is valuable in establishing a strong foundation to build a great life.

CHAPTER 27

TAKE CARE OF EACH OTHER

What would the world be like if we directed our energies away from divisiveness and hate and instead focused more on inclusion and joy?

During a trip to New York City a few years ago, my wife and I decided to ride the subway because it is the fastest way to get around there. We got into the subway car, sat down, and as the doors shut, I noticed two young men with drums. I turned to my wife and grumbled, "Darn, it's just my luck to be trapped in a subway and forced to listen to crappy music and then get hit up for a donation to boot." She chastised me, telling me that my negative attitude was unwarranted, and that the music would probably be great. As the drummers began to play, I was pleasantly surprised. They were excellent! Their soothing rhythm quickly changed my mood from hostile, aggressive, and edgy to peaceful and calm. As the doors opened and we filed out at the next station, I happily donated to them, grateful for the transformation I had experienced. I also reflected on how foolish I was to negatively prejudge them and how wise my wife was.

What made the moment hugely impactful for me was that as we exited the car, one of the drummers called out to everyone getting off saying, "Have a great day and take care of each other." The words "take care of each other" have stayed with me ever since. I think about them every day. This amazing message prompts me to ask myself why we continue to allow barriers such as race, religion, and nationality to divide us. What purpose do we serve by creating the seeds of an "us versus them" mentality?

I wonder how amazing the world would be if we could redirect many precious resources that are used to promote and support divisiveness, such as military and defense systems, spying technology, and the quest for political power, toward more productive and harmonious aims. What would happen if we invested more time, effort, and money into things that improve the human condition and that bring joy to people?

Because of that experience on the subway, I am more inclined to imagine a better, gentler, and more peaceful world. At a more basic level, I also rhetorically ask why we're so naturally vulnerable to being misguided into divisive thinking. Why are we inclined to judge each other so harshly, often without stopping to think or look closely at the reality of a situation? Why are so many of us enamored by leaders who see a divided world and fan those flames of division with their hostile rhetoric?

These things don't make much sense when you stop and think about them. When I look for answers, I go back to that day on the subway and remind myself of the simple and valuable lesson I learned from those drummers: take care of each other.

CHAPTER 28

THERE WILL ALWAYS BE HATRED

One of the most troubling aspects of human beings is our natural inclination to divide and hate. Although it is not logical, hatred has been part of humanity forever. And hatred, racism, and discrimination persist and take new forms in every generation. It is also a part of every generation to have movements aimed at eliminating hate. And, although the idea of eliminating hatred seems to be a worthy goal, based on the mountain of anecdotal evidence, it appears to be unachievable and maybe even laughably so.

Even worse, the effort to eradicate hatred often devolves into a call to curtail human freedoms, most commonly free speech. The leaders of these movements seem to believe that by inhibiting the language of hatred and intolerance, the world will be rid of the poison of hate. Not only is this naive but also it always backfires. The price of lost freedoms often lingers while the hate lives on. And, in this misguided effort to eliminate hate, once certain people are granted the power to choose what speech or actions are permitted and which are prohibited, the corrupting nature of power always leads to mass despair and, too frequently, more division and hatred.

I'm not suggesting that people accept hate or look the other way. I believe we should have zero tolerance for it on a personal level, ostracizing and eliminating all hateful people and behavior. This will contribute to a greater life. But on a societal scale, I'm highly skeptical of any organized efforts to eradicate hate.

EVERYONE IS A PHILOSOPHER, TEACHER, AND STUDENT

We've all heard the refrain from parents that they learn as much from their kids as they teach them. What they leave out is that this is primarily the lesson of patience, which, although important, can be quite a painful experience. That said, even the youngest and most inexperienced have things to teach the wisest among us. We are all teachers and we are all students.

We are also all philosophers, making decisions and living our lives based on a foundational philosophy that we've cobbled together since our earliest childhood. Most of us don't see ourselves as having a philosophy. Yet even in the absence of our own awareness, the philosophy is still there governing our lives. When and what we choose to eat, what we say or refrain from saying, whom we befriend, and our career decisions are all driven by our foundational life philosophy that we carry around with us and that has become our second nature. All our choices are perfect reflections of our life philosophy at that moment. And with each passing moment, and every bit of feedback that we get from the world, we get the opportunity to refine that philosophy, to modify it, and improve it. This philosophical foundation of ours is thus organic and alive, changing and growing with each of our experiences even when we don't even notice.

For example, one of my central life philosophies has long been rooted in the importance of being independent and not too much of a burden on others. I believe that this is the result of watching my mother struggle mightily to provide for my brother and me, and not wanting to be an extra burden on her. As I age, I make every effort to exercise daily and make healthy eating choices to ensure that my family doesn't have to bear the heavy weight of caring for a sick version of me. Clearly, there are no guarantees in life, and despite my best efforts, my health may fail, but I do all I can to achieve my objective. Yet, in seeming direct conflict with that line of reasoning, I have begun to learn recently that there is some beauty in dependence. I'm still pretty firmly in the camp of preferring independence, but I can see that dependence does foster giving by others, which creates deeper bonds between both the giver and the receiver that two very independent people may never get to enjoy.

Because we are all philosophers, it would be instructive to become more aware of our philosophy and how we arrived at it. I've found that being aware of my life philosophy and sharing it with others, including the writing of this book, enables me to challenge my ideas and update and modify them continually. This heightened awareness enables us to refine our philosophy by letting others examine and challenge it. Doing so creates the framework for continued personal growth.

CHAPTER 30

GIVING ADVICE IS SENSELESS

One of the by-products of achieving substantial career success early in my life is that others have frequently sought my advice. At the outset, being rather dumb and cocky, I gladly shared my opinions about what was best for others. Over time, I began to think more about this and realized that giving anything beyond general advice – such as don't lie, cheat, or steal – is mostly senseless.

Everyone needs to live their own life, make choices, derive both joy as well as suffering from the experiences resulting from those choices, and, most important, learn lessons to apply going forward. No two paths are alike, meaning that the choices best suited for you are likely not the best for anyone else. As I've gotten older, I appreciate how this holds true even for the parent and child relationship, where parents might be better served holding back on the advice-giving a bit more. Of course, when our kids are young, it is important to teach them, but at a certain age, we must step back in our role as teachers and allow them to live their own lives and follow their path.

Also, there is a natural difference between what an older and more experienced person knows and how they interpret the world and the views of a younger person. The older person may often see less merit in taking action, perhaps because their history with life's frustrations has taught them that the odds of failure in most endeavors are high. It would be tragic for younger people, on whom the world relies to be daring, creative, and even dreamy, to be influenced by this potentially crippling way of thinking. It would deprive the world of the naturally curious, ambitious, and creative energy that is more typical of youth, and that the world depends on for progress.

In the end, we are all on unique life journeys and ought to take great care before influencing the journey of another. I was born and lived my childhood in a small apartment in Yonkers. Those early experiences shaped my thoughts and interpretations of the world, contributing to my life choices. They still shape me and inform me to this day. No one, not even my children, is living my same life journey or has the same package of qualities and capabilities. That's why I believe sharing my perspectives with others must be done sparingly and judiciously. What might work for me is unlikely to work for another. Thus, anything other than choosing to provide general counsel such as "Don't lie, cheat, or steal or hurt others" runs the risk of impeding personal freedom of thought and the natural journey of life.

I am still asked for advice and guidance but am careful to share stories of my life and lessons that I've learned, enabling the listener to take away what resonates for them in a manner that may be valuable to them.

CHAPTER 31

LIFE IS AN IMPROV

We all have dreams, plans, and goals. The problem is that when we leave the front door of our homes and interact with others, we encounter people pursuing their own dreams and goals. That daily experience creates colliding agendas. People who can improvise well and adjust their plans to accommodate compromise with others are those who are most likely to enjoy healthy relationships and achieve great success.

Improvising and compromising is a challenge for most because it is human nature to focus our energy on achieving *our* goals and attending to *our* needs. In the competitive world that we live in, it is tough to accomplish those goals, and our inclination when facing resistance is to dig in even deeper and focus even more on our own game plan. In fact, we are often taught never to quit, to improvise, or to change direction in the face of resistance or challenge. Yet, this is directly at odds with life and the nature of the world itself, which constantly changes on every level. People who understand that and can balance being steadfast while still somehow remaining flexible will surely find greater fulfillment and more wins in life.

Paying careful attention to the world, with empathy for the needs of others, naturally leads to remaining flexible and adjusting our thinking and actions to create win-win outcomes. Competitiveness flows naturally when battling for resources, but balancing our resource needs with our soul's need for camaraderie and friendship aligns us with our fellow people and with the world itself.

I have lived and competed at the highest business levels and have seen too many of my peers chasing "I win, you lose" outcomes. These people have seemingly begrudged any dollars that may have evaded their pockets and found their way into the pockets of others. Although these "total wins" may feel good in a moment, those who pursue them too often end up alone, with few friendships or meaningful personal relationships. I've always worked hard in my career but wanted to win as a team, enjoying hugging and high-fiving my colleagues when we get into the end zone together.

Living with improvisation and empathy means living in harmony with others. Choosing to embrace change instead of living with unwavering rigidity is a critical prerequisite for growth, accomplishment, and happiness.

CHAPTER 32

KINDNESS AND GENEROSITY ARE THE HIGHEST LEVELS OF SELFISHNESS

I believe that everyone acts in their own best self-interest, in accordance with their interpretation of what that means. That is as it should be. Knowing this and anticipating how different people view what is in their best interests can be very helpful in business and life.

Some might suggest that this is an acceptance of people's selfishness, and indeed it is. However, there are different kinds of selfishness. I call the one that we are most familiar with and generally deride "unenlightened selfishness," whereby a person pursues their immediate, short-term interests without regard for any longer-term ramifications. Another more benevolent kind is "long-term selfishness," whereby we trade off short-term glory for some larger benefit down the road. The ultimate level of selfishness is "enlightened selfishness," where we derive significant joy from being of service to another, exceeding the joy of personal consumption or gain.

I recall my mom bringing home groceries, which always included a twelve-pack of mini-cereal boxes. My brother Joe and I would quarrel, bargain, and negotiate over who would get the best ones, which invariably were the ones with the most sugar, and who would get stuck with the booby prizes like Cheerios or Corn Flakes. Initially, we'd resort to whatever advantages we had, whether it was size and force or manipulative skills, to win the right boxes. Over time, as the older brother, I realized that if I were kind to my brother and gave him the first choice, I'd still get my share of sugar. The other equally important benefit was that I'd look gracious and considerate to my mom, building up goodwill that I could cash in at a later time, a version of long-term selfishness. In those rare sibling moments when the bickering gave way to love, I'd actually want my brother to have the most desirable cereal choices because seeing him happy gave me greater satisfaction than eating the cereal myself. In time, I even learned to enjoy Cheerios and Corn Flakes, albeit with some fruit on top. This was my introduction to enlightened selfishness.

The concept of selfishness is misunderstood and thus given a blanket bad rap. Every single person will always act in their best interest. We are hardwired this way. Kind people who act in a manner we label unselfish are still acting selfishly. However, they've learned that there is an even greater joy to sharing and giving than there is in consuming. In fact, if personal joy or the avoidance of sadness is one's goal, I would tell you that giving or focusing on others rather than yourself is a sure-fire way to accomplish this goal. I believe that sadness comes mostly from self-pity, which is a state that involves a complete inward focus on oneself rather than an outward one on others.

CHAPTER 33

MASTERY IS SIMPLICITY

A quote attributed to the late comedian W. C. Fields reads, "If you can't dazzle them with brilliance, baffle them with bullshit." It's a remarkable insight that defines great people versus pretenders, or those who have not yet attained mastery. In my career, I've heard the term *genius* applied to many but have only encountered a precious few who live up to that billing. The rest are very good actors.

In many situations, perhaps a college professor lecturing or a politician describing budget deficits, we've all felt lost and have assumed that the speaker is highly competent with an advanced mastery of the subject material. I've learned that often the opposite is true. Regardless of the subject, grandiose and overly complicated language uttered to try and impress an audience is a red flag that may be little more than a poor attempt to cover up a lack of deep understanding and mastery of a subject.

Think about people you enjoy listening to or reading about and ask yourself what they have in common. Charlie Munger, Elon Musk, and Charles Barkley are fine examples of people in the public domain who have deep domain expertise but can communicate their insights in a manner that hits home for every listener, regardless of the level of sophistication. These people and many others like them have perfected the art of taking complicated subjects where they have significant expertise, and distilling them to their simplest terms when communicating, reflecting their extreme subject mastery.

When you find yourself listening to someone and scratching your head in confusion, it may be that the speaker is not quite the master they are promoted to be. True masters have a deep grasp of their subject matter and are self-aware enough to know that their audience does not. They take time to communicate with passion and power and effectively translate complex ideas into easy-to-understand concepts.

Simplicity is mastery, whereas complexity unexplained is often a reflection that those doing the talking don't actually have a solid grasp on their subject matter. Simplicity is earned through deep immersion into a subject and understanding how to best transfer that knowledge to others. We live in a time when too many people are in a rush, look for shortcuts, and are not shy to speak as though they have expertise. That devalues real knowledge and competence and deprives the world of wisdom from those who can teach and share valuable insights. These frauds and their followers often flame out in one form or another. Being judicious before speaking and while listening will help guide one toward a life with better outcomes.

CHAPTER 34

THE BEST IDEAS
SURVIVE OPEN DEBATE

There should be no taboos. All ideas should be open
to challenges that produce the best possible thinking. When I see intolerance of debate or a prohibi-
tion against articulating opposing points of view, that
is a strong indication that the idea being espoused and
protected is probably flawed. This problem has grown
significantly of late in a hyper sensitive world that is
quick to ostracize anyone who dares to question an
accepted way of thinking.

For example, as the *New York Times* reported in April 2023, students
at Stanford Law School disrupted a conservative federal judge who
had been invited to talk at the school. Some students felt like they
didn't even need to hear and debate the views of this conservative
justice. That seems contrary to the foundations of law school, where
the hardest arguments have to be made and debated openly, and that's
exactly what the dean said in a 10-page memo. These kinds of issues
are arising at schools across the country, where, apparently, many students and teachers only want to hear what they already believe.

One of the significant advantages of a society that embraces free speech is that its citizens can all get smarter from the exchange and debate on disparate ideas. The example I cite is merely a symptom of a larger societal problem, where we are quick to accuse and belittle those with different points of view. Everyone suffers when we can't engage in civil discourse that creates a better understanding and critical exchange of ideas.

Every person lives according to a unique narrative that was formed based on experiences and observations. This narrative is imperfect because any one's perspectives are, by definition, limited. It is impossible for one individual to see or know everything. It is only by engaging with others and listening with an open mind that we are better positioned to modify and improve our narrative.

CHAPTER 35

THE RIPPLE EFFECT

A well-known Jewish teaching states that to save or to have a positive impact on a single life is as though you've saved the whole world. I had dismissed this as a nonsensical exaggeration in my youth. But now, I see the power of what I call the ripple effect. By influencing just one single person, we have the potential to see the positive effects ripple through the world and reach untold numbers of people.

We don't need a huge audience or millions of friends or followers on social media. If we touch a single person or a select few, they may recount the impact to others, and that ripple can potentially spread throughout much of the world. The math is amazing. If you persuade only 15 friends and they each can persuade another 15, by the time this has taken place just eight times you'll reach more than 2.5 billion people! Your reach is far greater than you imagine. Be a role model, even if you think you're not powerful or can't reach many people.

Creating a powerful ripple effect is actually simple, and we have those opportunities continuously throughout the day. For example, what is the potential ripple effect of tipping a server generously? In this instance, it is easy to imagine the grateful server bringing their customers a different and kinder spirit throughout the day. Those patrons touched by that cheer are more likely to pass it on as they go about their lives. So, a gesture as small as a single generous tip can literally affect millions.

Consider the ripple effect potential in all of your daily interactions with others. When you choose to live this way, your actions may reverberate worldwide, adding value to lives far beyond your circle.

CHAPTER 36

SEXUALITY AND THE IMPORTANCE OF SEXUAL ENERGY

I once heard Dave Chappelle tell a story about how early in his career he used to perform on weekends in a small club in New York City owned by a drug dealer. One Saturday night after his show, the dealer came to his dressing room and gave him a paper bag filled with $25,000 in cash as a bonus for a great performance. Chappelle recounted how nervous and paranoid he was late at night, riding the subway home to his sketchy Brooklyn neighborhood with that prize in his backpack. As he explained, at that moment he understood what it is like to be a woman . . . always on guard.

As he shared this story, I also understood, perhaps for the first time, how challenging it is to be a woman, living in a world where men are hardwired to crave them for procreation. I don't think that men fully appreciate the burden that women face, walking around daily and being lusted after and objectified. This story was very moving for me, and it helped me relate to women much better. There is so much tension, confusion, and negative energy about sex and sexuality, which is entirely at odds with its central role in creating life itself, and as a source of great joy.

Human sexuality is quite complicated. We all know that sex plays a central role in perpetuating human life, and our roles as mothers and fathers are rooted in sexuality. But sex is also more than procreation. The promise of sex is a great stimulant for bliss, excitement, playfulness, and creativity for men and women. Taoists believe that sexual energy is the root of all human creativity and productivity, which makes intuitive sense to me.

Sexuality and all that accompanies it, including flirting, courtship, and discovery, are great fun. You didn't need to tell the youth in my generation this. We all knew it, and there was no disputing it. As I've aged, I've observed that as people get older, they lose their sexuality. I don't pretend to know the precise reason, and I'm sure many factors contribute. I do believe that the absence of healthy sexual energy not only leads to broken homes and disappointing relationships but also, I believe, contributes to a diminished human spirit with less gusto for life. It doesn't have to be this way. Sexual vibrancy is a wonderful hallmark of a great and joyful life. To achieve this, both partners must choose to maintain sexual vibrancy.

CHAPTER 37

EMOTIONS OFTEN BLOCK TRUTH

The issue of human emotions is quite complicated. We are emotional. That is a fact. Some people are more emotional, and some are less. Our unique backgrounds create different positive and negative emotional triggers for each of us. We also react to stimuli with different types and levels of intensity, resulting in our unique human existence.

If joy and tranquility are core life goals, which I'll go out on a limb and guess they are for most, then emotional reactions that conflict with that desire are not helpful. They should be managed with great care. Negative emotions are destructive and lead us to the opposite state of mind. Emotional reactions without the benefit of reasoning will hurt others and destroy relationships.

I am not suggesting that we ignore or repress our emotions, but instead that we master them, giving them weight and consideration but only in the context of rational thinking. Emotions are the opposite of calm and reasoned thinking, making this balancing act an ongoing internal tug of war. Mastering our lives generally requires us to be aware of and to master our emotions while also focusing on facts and reality to the greatest extent possible, with a constant eye toward achieving the desired outcome. Sometimes I ask someone who has reacted emotionally what their desired endgame is. Occasionally, this returns the mood to a rational one yet at other times further infuriates the individual. I think keeping an eye on the prize – the desired outcome – is a healthy way to manage emotional surges.

In the central Jewish prayer, the Shema, which is directly excerpted from the Torah, or the Old Testament, there is a line from God that directs man to "not stray after your heart or your eyes, following your sinful desires." Humans, like all animals, feel. Yet, humans are alone in the animal kingdom to have the ability to override our instincts and emotions with reason. History has shown that without the balance of reason, we risk descending to a level of emotionally influenced behaviors that are suboptimal at best and dangerous, and even murderous, at worst.

CHAPTER 38

WE ALL SCREW UP

We can never be fully prepared for a new day, challenge, or situation. That's what makes life interesting, but it also means that every one of us will screw up from time to time. Who among us feels they get parenting entirely right or are a perfect spouse? Life is full of trials and errors. We all make mistakes, and we all fail often. The key is to learn and grow.

If we embrace these failures and mistakes rather than try to sweep them under the rug or blame them on bad luck, they can be our best teachers. We must be proud of them and speak of them openly to share our lessons with others and also to better lock in what we have learned. When we don't own our mistakes and remind ourselves of the lessons that we've learned, we risk repeating them. Failures are forgivable if we're sure we gave all we had and learned what we could from the experience. Failures experienced without lessons learned are tragic missed opportunities and likely mean that we'll experience similar failures down the road. I know that I won't do business with people who can't comfortably recount their past failures and speak to the lessons they've learned. Indeed, I don't find those people attractive in any way.

Many young people, especially the smarter ones, are quite sure of themselves. I recall being supremely confident that I had just about everything figured out when I was younger. I'm sure I wasn't the only one. Yet with time, it is common to look back at our past cocksure selves as having been idiots. Believe it or not, this is a super-healthy sign. It means having lived life and pursued experiences, trying and failing often. It also means setting aside the ego to accept life lessons and committing to ongoing learning and improvement.

One of the great things that I learned from my folks was that smart people mostly listen and that the smartest ones are those with all the questions, not the answers. I find it problematic that we live in a society where we are encouraged to appear to know it all and to be ashamed of our flaws, mistakes, and failures. Too many people are unwilling to admit their mistakes and are uncomfortable saying they were wrong or even ever apologizing. This results in people making bad choices, including avoiding risks and living inside the herd for fear of being wrong. It also leads to blaming others for failures and mistakes rather than accepting responsibility, which prevents learning for the actor and causes undue pain for others.

When I speak publicly, I am apt to prompt the audience to ask themselves what ideas each of them has held as having been true earlier in their lives and have now changed their mind on to such a degree that they accept the opposite as either being valid or at least worthy of consideration. That is something all of us should be asking ourselves regularly. If the answer is "nothing," then I suggest thinking hard about that and wondering whether it is due to having been born with perfect knowledge or simply never having learned a thing. I'd venture that the answer is not the former.

In sum, we can't learn too much from success, just a reinforcement of things that we already know and do quite well. But the opportunity to learn from failures and disappointments is profound. Being dishonest and not acknowledging mistakes, or not apologizing, reflecting, or learning means not growing. We will all screw up and have regular opportunities to learn from our mistakes, and thus to grow and to improve. A life of learning, growth, and humility is a great and fulfilling life.

CHAPTER 39

THE KID IN THE PLAYGROUND

I had a great childhood, spending countless hours and days with my friends in the playground and sports fields or playing board games like Monopoly, Life, and other popular games of the day. I didn't realize it then, but those days spent playing games would directly affect me later in life.

Once I entered the workplace, I needed to figure out how to get along with adults. As my career reached higher levels, this challenge grew as I began interacting with highly successful people in the business world. I was intimidated by these people who had achieved so much and who clearly knew a lot more about almost everything than I did. Then, I figured out a hack of sorts that worked well. I realized that, at our essence, we are all just versions of the kid that we once were in the playground. Armed with this insight, I learned how to remain at ease and to demystify those intimidatingly successful people by relating to that child that I imagined was at their core.

In many ways, the state of being an adult is unnatural, often shrouded by masks that we've donned to become someone whom we believe others will respect, admire, or even fear. Our natural state occurs at birth and I don't think that it is too big a stretch to suggest that everything else since is a learned and practiced act. Ultimately, these masks that we all wear obscure our true selves and, most of all, they conceal the parts of us that are most lovely and endearing. They hide our beauty and our uniqueness.

In my 30s, due to my young career success, I got to meet iconic figures in the business world and became close personal friends with some, including Alfred Taubman, who created the modern-day indoor mall, and the oil tycoon Marvin Davis, who later became the owner of Fox Studios. These men were decades older and far more accomplished than I was. Initially, it was a bit intimidating being around them, but as we became closer and they allowed me to see more of their true selves, I realized how they frequently wore masks in public, playing the part of moguls and reaping the benefits, which included admiration and status.

However, wearing these masks also came at a cost. They hid their lovable and playful essence from many, and surely inhibited relationships and joy that could only have been had with the individual living behind the masks. Because they let me see behind the mask, I got to know these titans for the beautiful, fun, and even gentle human beings that they really were. I got to know the child that was at their essence and that resided in them even into their later years. That enabled me to have a special relationship with them and I will always appreciate that they trusted me enough to take their masks off for me. Their friendships were huge blessings.

If you are intimidated or uncomfortable around certain people or situations, imagine those people as kids in the playground. I think you'll find they aren't so different from you, and that will put your mind at ease when you understand the rest is just a learned and practiced act. Invariably, this will also lead you to enjoy more rewarding and deeper relationships.

CHAPTER 40

THE UNIQUE LOVE OF A PARENT

Parents are special and deserve everything from their children, which is probably why the honoring of parents is one of the Ten Commandments. As I teach my kids, if you can't be nice to me, the person who is there for you always and without condition or agenda, who on earth can you be nice to?

There is no love comparable to the love that a parent has for their child. That love is uniquely pure and unconditional. If children understood this, they'd lean on and appreciate their parents much more. They would ask their parents all types of questions, frequently seeking out their knowledge and counsel, comforted that parents are the only ones on earth who could respond without any competing agendas to the child's best interest.

Also, so much of who we are emanates from our earliest years, which we have a poor or even no recollection of. Parents are the only ones who have witnessed us from our earliest moments and have seen us grow over time. We would have a so much better understanding of ourselves and thus be better able to grow and function optimally if we could be properly informed about ourselves and our development with the perspective of those formative years.

I have had the privilege of parenting five children and a strong hand in mentoring a few other young men and women in a parent-like manner. Like all parents, I've made my share of mistakes. My extreme love led me to be overindulgent at times. Before some serious personal growth, my natural impatience and quick temper led me to act in ways that I would quickly regret. But I've always taken the responsibility of parenting seriously, and as my mother did with me, I have always valued treating my kids with great respect. I tried to explain and teach when guiding, criticizing, or even punishing. I also strived to be real, human, and approachable, knowing that my best chance at teaching is through having my kids observe me and my life's choices and actions, not simply hearing lectures.

The thing is that we're not all parents, but we are all children of parents. So, in addressing this topic, my primary focus is on my role and responsibility as a son. Even though my parents have long since passed on from this world, I feel a daily obligation to honor them. I feel their presence in my life always and want to have them be proud of how I honor their legacy through all of my deeds. This includes, of course, how I parent their precious grandchildren. This desire to honor my parents, as much as anything else, propels me to make the choices that I believe lead a person to greatness.

I must add here that obviously not all parents show this special love easily, or even at all. I understand that many children are abandoned and feel unloved in this world. To this I must again talk to the children in each of us, rather than the parent, and ask you to forgive your parent and if possible to give that person another chance, no matter how many chances you've given them before. The love is there, I promise you, although it may be blocked.

When I met my wife Marisol, she had not had a relationship with her dad for more than a decade. He had left her and the family when she was a teenager. When she tried to reconnect with him in her 20s he rebuffed her, and she gave up on him. At that time, I was freshly divorced from my first wife and was suffering from the fear and the reality of being disconnected from my two beautiful children. From that perspective, I had tremendous empathy for my wife and her father, knowing that their lives would be so much better if they reconciled. So, despite only having known her for about six months, I arranged for her father to come to California from Venezuela and to knock on our front door and surprise her for her birthday. That led to the hoped-for reconciliation, and they enjoyed a close relationship for the next 21 years until his passing.

CHAPTER 41

COMFORT IN THE HERD

Humans are herd animals. We take comfort surrounding ourselves with people who reinforce our beliefs, aiming to feel less alone and more relevant as part of a larger group. Finding comfort in the herd plays out in many ways. We are constantly trying to persuade others to see things our way, whether about admiring our new car, agreeing with us about our favorite restaurant and sports teams, or our political opinions.

The unfortunate consequence of this thinking is that too many people recalibrate their wants, their goals, and their dreams to align with what others want, and especially with the tastes of the so-called popular people – celebrities, athletes, entertainers, and other cultural icons. In this process, we sacrifice what we might truly want for the trade-off of fitting in. This desire to fit in or to be cool and accepted by the "in crowd" invariably will make us feel more isolated and unfulfilled, chasing an imagined ideal that is not real, not attainable, nor what our soul truly yearns for. To experience happiness we must first honestly identify and pursue the things that we actually desire.

Media, including traditional, social media, marketing, and also politics, have preyed on and benefited immensely from the human inclination to find comfort in a herd by pandering to that inclination. As a result of their efforts, there is now an almost unbridgeable chasm of polarization that divides us. A functional society cannot exist with such a divide, but this situation can only change when we learn to stand comfortably on our own two feet.

If you've been alive for a while, you may have noticed major financial dislocations recurring cyclically, typically every 7 to 10 years. As a financial market expert, I can tell you that one of the major contributors to this recurring phenomenon is people's inclination toward herd thinking and herd action. Everyone becomes bullish and complacent about risk until the beginning of a downturn. At that point, everyone becomes bearish all at once. Significant fortunes have been made and will continue to be made by those who remain discerning and less vulnerable to the emotions associated with such herd behavior, and who have the courage to go in the opposite direction of the herd.

Just as is true for the investment world, greatness means being special or different and, by definition, must occur outside of the herd. Daring to be great takes a rare degree of courage and a willingness to be alone. Individuals willing to live outside of the herd are society's real change agents. They shun the comfort of the herd in favor of living a challenging and fulfilling life. That directly conflicts with those who prefer the "go along to get along" mindset, a core part of the herd mentality that gravitates to comfort and the safety of the status quo.

A good test of whether someone lives outside of the herd and is a change agent is by how popular they are. It is difficult for real change agents to be broadly embraced. Their efforts will naturally be opposed by those who continue to benefit from the perpetuation of the status quo and those who might benefit from change but have been brainwashed to stay inside of the herd. Because change is uncomfortable for most, agents of change naturally make most people a bit uncomfortable. It seems that each aspiring political leader promises to be a change agent, but most just want to have power and find their spot among the elite. They don't want to change anything, nor do they have the stomach for handling the natural enmity that such a path ensures.

CHAPTER 42

INERTIA DESTROYS, ALWAYS GO

There is probably nothing more prevalent than the pull of inertia and we can see its harmful results daily in nearly all facets of life. Most of us complain often about many things, yet we do little to insist on or to bring about any change. Indeed, our silence makes us complicit in perpetuating bad situations.

We send our kids to schools whose curriculums resemble those from more than 50 years ago, dooming so many of our children to a horrible and near-worthless school experience. We visit doctors who evaluate our health and guide us in our health care and, too often, continue to embrace old ideas and treatments. They will seemingly go to great lengths to avoid even considering newer ideas and often prescribe medications that address our symptoms but ignore the root causes. We're smart enough to know that this is not right. So much information is out there and available to us. Yet, mostly, we do nothing. The list of systemic inertia goes on and on.

On a physical level, the allure of the sofa in opposition to exercise and activity is amazingly powerful. People are great at being lazy and squandering opportunities to challenge themselves and others to be better. Even more alarming, we are inclined to repel anyone who challenges us and espouses change.

When young people ask me for career advice, I mostly tell them just to do something – anything – and then they can figure out on the fly how to improvise and optimize. Long ago, I developed a personal philosophy I call "Always Go." As the words imply, this would be the opposite of inertia and is a constant call to action. Simply put, movement or action leads to good things, and the absence of movement and action leads to nothing.

Related to this call to action is persistence in the face of failure or severe challenge. My dear friend Irving Azoff is a giant in the music and entertainment industry. In the 30 years that I've known Irving, I've witnessed how he climbed back up to the top of the mountain in his field after dramatically falling from that peak decades earlier. When we'd recount our frequent failures along the way to one another, he'd say to me, "You've got to dig a lot of dry holes," which meant that working through disappointment and failure were the key prerequisites to any meaningful achievement. Irving's attitude and success constantly inspire me whenever I set out to achieve anything. I remind myself every time I experience failure and disappointment, I only lose when I've decided to stop trying.

CHAPTER 43

More Is Not Better

For the past few centuries, America has led the world in many ways in introducing ideology, ideas, and technology. The historic commitment to personal liberty and a free market that fosters social mobility has been positive. Other contributions, such as the notion that "more is better," have been tragic. This way of thinking, rooted in envy and jealousy, moves people away from finding what is right or best for them and instead blindly pursuing more for its own sake.

This gluttony is one of the so-called seven deadly sins and for good reason. Pursuing more money, more square footage, more and costlier material things, larger portions of food on our plates, and even artificially larger body parts like lips or rear ends are all great examples of the misguided notion that more is better. People always pay a big price and make unwitting sacrifices for the unbridled pursuit of more. Mostly, they become disconnected with their true essence, as the pursuit of more is a version of chasing the fool's gold of external esteem at the expense of knowing and ultimately admiring oneself.

I have a friend and business mentor who, in his elder years, confessed in tears that despite his massive wealth, renown, and power, his life was a total failure. Here, in his later years, he realized that he desperately craved love and that he had sacrificed that and much else for the pursuit of things that in reflection were worth very little. His career success had inspired envy and fear in others but never love or affection. Near the end of his life, he wept at how lonely his life journey had been. I must say that this was among the saddest moments that I've ever witnessed, and it shook me.

There are many dimensions to fulfillment and achievement. Material security and the joy that it brings is only one of those. A great life achieves greatness in many ways. Love, genuine relationships, health, purpose, and a sense of being of service are also important, but they all require that we invest in them. Excesses in one area often create a deficit in others, which is bound to leave us with sentiments like that of my friend.

PART THREE

THE FOUNDATIONS OF A GREAT SOCIETY

CHAPTER 44

THE IMPORTANCE OF TIMING

Timing affects everything. I learned this lesson well in my career, along with the equally important lesson of humility. The early stage of my career was a meteoric success. By the time I was in my 30s, I was at the top of the US finance and real estate industries. Then, things changed abruptly. At the time, I viewed this moment as a temporary bump in the road. I was young and knew that I was talented and willing to work hard, so I just assumed I would regain my prior career perch in short order.

More than two decades later, more experienced, wiser, more well known, and as hardworking as ever, I have achieved success but that prior peak has not yet been revisited as of this writing. I learned that hard work, persistence, and talent do ensure success but that the level of success is uncertain and largely depends on timing.

Mammoth successes require timing to be just right, in addition to all the other things that need to be in place. A great effort by talented people who are out of sync with the times is unlikely to bring superior results. But such an effort that is relevant for the time, or one that is novel or revolutionary, will have a much more significant outcome. When Ray Kroc introduced McDonald's, he introduced fast food to a nation that was just becoming pressed for time and had less interest in preparing and eating at home than that of previous generations. Kroc and McDonald's caught the nascent inclination of eating out and perfectly rode the crest of its increasing popularity to become the mega-success that the world knows today. There would be few who would argue that if Kroc came along even five years sooner when every American family treasured their family meals at home, and women took great pride in their culinary contributions to the family, he would likely have never achieved the same level of success.

A person's skills and talents are also rewarded differently depending on whether they are part of something operating at peak relevancy and whether they've found the right complements for their skills. For example, without Steve Jobs's vision and marketing talents, Apple cofounder Steve Wozniak's talents as a great programmer would not have likely been as highly rewarded. They needed each other, and had they not met, or if they had come around a decade earlier before there was any appetite for the products that made them so successful, they probably wouldn't have found anywhere near the level of success that they did in launching Apple.

When weighing choices about career, relationships, and other important life decisions, carefully consider timing as part of your process. Ask yourself if what you are endeavoring to do is in harmony with the world and the direction that you see it progressing. Deciding what to do based on your desires or skills is only part of the equation. Evaluating the timeliness and the relevance of the mission is at least as important and can often spell the difference between massive success and average outcomes.

CHAPTER 45

TRUSTING OUR INSTINCTS

None of us knows everything, and overall, we know very little. However, like all animals, humans have great instincts. My mom taught me that our instincts are a lot like a muscle. The more we rely on them for our decision-making, the stronger they become and the more in tune we get with them. On the flipside, the less we trust our instincts and the more we doubt ourselves, the hazier our connection to that inner voice becomes and the less available it will be to us down the road.

Our lives involve making decisions all day, every day, and always with imperfect information. Having well-honed instincts is a huge asset when choosing how to live. However, we don't always get things right, and knowing when we've placed ourselves on the wrong path and being bold enough to make quick changes is also important. In this very confusing life, with no real guidebook and only ourselves to rely on, it's comforting to have a deep relationship with our native instinct, honed with each challenge and decision.

Another aspect of using our instincts when facing decisions involves asking ourselves if something has what I call *the ring of truth*. When considering something, we must ask ourselves if it stands up to the scrutiny of common sense. For example, my family purchased a newly constructed home in Mexico. Unfortunately, the faucets produced only warm water even when we turned on the cold water. When we complained, the builder told us that this was because Baja California is a hot weather climate. I'm not a home building expert, but I know that I've lived in warm climates and in less well-appointed dwellings where one's expectations of quality of construction might be lower than for the more costly home I had just purchased. I never had a problem getting cold water before, so this builder's explanation failed the ring-of-truth test.

Among the biggest ring-of-truth failures takes place annually in Washington, DC, when politicians produce budgets that involve spending trillions of dollars while telling citizens that it will not cost us a thing. Then, with massive deficits built up from years of spending more than they've taken from us in taxes, politicians tell us that the resulting deficits don't mean a thing. This obviously makes no sense. Yet, as a society, we fail to apply the ring-of-truth test while the deficits grow and the eventual price that we'll pay for reconciliation grows.

In my world of finance, I see common sense violated every day and in many ways. That includes what investments people make, whom they trust to manage their money, how they compensate them, and decisions of when to buy and sell.

Making smart choices is the foundation of living a great life. There are so many confusing voices, many that are aimed at manipulating us to make choices that are beneficial to them and often contradictory to our own best interests. Trusting and honing our native instincts and applying the ring-of-truth test are valuable ways to navigate our way through the noise and find our best path.

CHAPTER 46

FREEDOM

Freedom is a word,
With a complex meaning.
Most of us get it wrong.
And are forever needing.
You've got the freedom to move,
And the freedom to speak,
But you don't notice the strait
jacket and muzzle,
Your situation is actually quite
bleak.
Say what's on your mind,
That's a dare.
Do you have the courage?
Is it worth the fare?
Go vote, you schmuck.
All the celebrities tell you to.
But step out of line too loudly,
And you'll learn the limits of
what you can do.
What risks for your freedom?
To be monitored and tracked for
our own good.

What price to be paid?
More bombs and less food.
Let's invade a small country,
They need some freedom.
Our bombs and our bullets,
They will surely welcome.
Trade your time for money,
Or drink and beg like bums.
All value is debased,
As the printing press hums.
Trust the government to manage
your life?
They can't even deliver the mail.
The best they can do,
Is to run a big jail.
Fear is our governor,
We wish to belong.
Be true to your spirit,
Anything else is all wrong.

CHAPTER 47

MOST OF US NEVER NOTICE

A few years ago, during the Global Financial Crisis of 2008, otherwise known as the GFC or in some circles the Great Recession, I was walking through Grand Central Terminal, traveling from the subway to my office. In the terminal's main hall, which is a true work of art, I passed by a massive man dressed in complete US military attire that included a thick bullet-proof vest and an automatic rifle. He was dressed for the battlefield as he mingled almost naturally among the hundreds of civilians in their work attire. While I'd seen this added security before as a result of the 9/11 bombing and perhaps concerns related to the GFC, it hit me differently that day, and I started thinking how desensitized we've become to dramatic changes that in times past would have been inconceivable.

As you go about your day, think about how different your world is now from even 5 or 10 years ago. The speed and breadth at which the internet, computers, smartphones, robotics, and medical breakthroughs have transformed our lives is astounding. Similarly, we've also seen major shifts in thinking about things as far-ranging as climate issues, racial divisions, global conflicts, corruption, weak leadership, and law enforcement.

Some of these changes have been dramatic, initiated by triggering events like the GFC, but for the most part, changes are incremental and mostly go unnoticed. The speed at which news is now disseminated captures our full attention in increasingly shorter time frames. We're being bombarded with so much change that sometimes these changes lose contextual meaning. Unfortunately, the most troubling part of this shift is that we're more prone than ever before to accept negative changes as a normal part of life. We have lowered our standard of what we're willing to accept, and to me, that spells trouble in the long term for individuals and for our society as a whole.

As a guy who's spent his career in finance, one of the things that comes to mind as I reflect on this is the government's rather recent move to become deeply involved in the markets, especially through the more aggressive use of monetary policies such as quantitative easing by central bankers. You may not be familiar with quantitative easing, so a short history lesson here might be helpful.

In November 2008, during the most serious market panic in modern times, the Federal Reserve engaged in a policy of quantitative easing, or QE. QE is the process that involves the Fed printing money and introducing it into the market by purchasing mortgage-backed securities and US Treasury bonds. So, if it's still not completely clear, this is the process by which money is conjured out of thin air by our government and then injected into the system. Until the GFC, QE had not been used by the Fed in my lifetime or in modern times. Given the extreme level of manipulation that it represents, QE was a tool that most market participants until that moment had never even imagined being used. Fear that its use might cause normal people to become loathe to accept paper currency as value in exchange for goods or services was something that had long kept this genie in his bottle.

Fortunately, despite its aggressive use in the 15 years since the GFC, people's level of complacency has prevented such fears from being realized. The sheep, as we're generally thought of by those in power, have remained calm and asleep. Outside of people like me who pay close attention to financial markets, most have not noticed that any of this was happening, nor could they understand the massive impact it has had in their everyday lives. By the time the QE policy ended in 2022, the Fed had conjured nearly $8 trillion of new money out of thin air, and the impact on everyone's lives has been quite large. Prices of most everything, perhaps most meaningfully food and gas, soared (an effect commonly referred to as inflation) and higher interest rates on mortgages, car loans, credit card rates, and small business loans have strained family budgets and threaten the nation's economic future.

QE and the increased governmental intrusion on markets of the past two decades has had a major impact on the lives of all Americans and non-Americans, too. Yet over time, most people have accepted it and the consequences as being the new normal. Over the past five decades, the government has also deepened its involvement in many other aspects of life, including healthcare, education, and trade. These always began as temporary intrusions or quick fixes, but once the government touches a part of society, it rarely retreats. This is the nature of government. I know it is difficult to even imagine, but the concept of a national income tax was a temporary one introduced in the US in 1861 to finance the Civil War. Can you imagine?

As a father of five children, I've realized that this higher level of government oversight and involvement is just one of many differences my children and their peers will know going forward. With technology that can monitor everything and everyone now available, I wonder how much further things will go before we collectively choose to wake up and challenge things.

CHAPTER 48

PRO-CYCLICALITY CAN BE CRUSHING

Much of the world is pro-cyclical. That is to say that we are mostly organized to follow norms and to follow each other wherever that leads. We are calibrated to follow, and thus to be synchronized. We hear information and because we're all human, we tend to react to things in similar ways. This herd behavior creates and reinforces all types of cycles, including those in business, economic, political, fashion, culture, music, and more.

Exacerbating this pro-cyclicality is the desire of so-called leaders to appease their flock and to avoid rocking the boat. These leaders, whose primary objective is generally to remain in power, are astute enough to understand that they have little to gain by taking positions that are opposite to conventional thinking. This would be deemed to be controversial and therefore jeopardize their status as leaders. Thus, they are inclined to take positions that simply reinforce the herd mentality, making the herd more confident of and committed to their path regardless of the merit of the path being taken.

A great example of this was the stance of Ben Bernanke while chairman of the Federal Reserve Bank in 2007. As the world economy was about to go off a proverbial cliff, Bernanke, the principal economic leader of the nation, famously gave the all-clear sign when he said that the risks from housing excesses to the broader economy were limited and that things would not be too bad. He obviously didn't want to upset people by telling them the truth, preferring happy talk instead. Months later, the world was in the worst global financial crisis since the Great Depression. Bernanke's happy talk didn't help anyone prepare themselves, and as a result the impact of the downturn was surely far more painful than it otherwise could have been.

People will choose leaders with whom they're comfortable, which pretty much excludes anyone who thinks out of the box or is willing to risk their status as leaders to do or say the right thing. So instead, we end up with leaders who parrot back to us what polls reflect is our consensus. In the most benign cases, these leaders achieve nothing good, and at their worst, they lead us off cliffs. I've enjoyed being a contrarian, thinking naturally that if there is a consensus, the opposite is probably true. This has led me to mostly be right and ahead of the pack about many large things, financial or otherwise, but at times can also feel a bit lonely.

CHAPTER 49

RACISM AND DISCRIMINATION ARE THE DOMAIN OF THE DUMB

We are all human. This is the only real categorization that we should apply to one another. And yet, we witness daily attempts to classify and divide us further. No matter what religious or racial group, sexual preference, gender, where you were born and raised, or your level of wealth or education, you are a unique human being who deserves to be treated with respect.

We all belong to different groups based on our commonalities and preferences, but we should not simply ascribe group tendencies blindly to each member of a group or prejudge people on that basis. Every group includes people who are kind and those who are not, those who are hostile and others who are passive, some who are more intelligent or physically attractive than others. No group of people is perfect or superior or inferior to other groups.

Martin Luther King Jr. spoke about dreaming of the day when his kids would be "judged not by the color of their skin but by the content of their character." I am in the same camp. None of the individual groupings beyond the classification of "human being" should matter.

I see those who label, judge, and stereotype others as being among our world's lesser lights – they are morons. I'm inclined to at least accept them, if not forgive them, due to their obvious intellectual limitations. I can only hope that they get smarter. What I cannot grasp is the senseless perpetuation of these groupings by those who are in the groups and who insist on being continually identified by their race, gender, religion, skin color, sexual preference, birthplace, or other identifiers. To me, they are allowing those lesser lights with their limited intelligence to define who they are. This makes no sense at all to me. Of course, we are tribal, too, so perpetuating and sharing our tribal heritages is delightful. However, when we allow ourselves to be goaded into a level of tribal separation that somehow defines us as being different from others in all of the human qualities, I think that is problematic.

Everyone deserves identical human rights, no more or less than anyone else. In my mind, there should not be a call for rights by or for any one group. I believe that this only reinforces the misguided notion that the groupings themselves are legitimate when in fact they are not at all.

CHAPTER 50

DEMOCRACY DEPENDS ON EDUCATION

Democracy depends on a voter population that is discerning, informed, and educated and on people who understand the lessons of history and can vote for what is best for society. Conversely, in a one-person/one-vote democracy like we have in the US, if most voters are uninformed and uneducated, our society stands a much greater chance of getting unqualified leadership.

US school statistics on grade-level literacy and math competence have been heading in the wrong direction for years. This has happened primarily because we have turned our backs on the education system that we depend on to produce competent young men and women to select among themselves who shall lead the country wisely. The result is that too large of a percentage of our population enters adulthood poorly prepared to produce any value in the working world, incapable of supporting themselves or their family, and completely unprepared for the responsibility of selecting the nation's leaders.

Just as global competition heated up in recent decades, the US continually lowered academic standards in our public schools, producing poorly educated graduates at an alarming rate. A recent editorial in

EducationWeek talked about how lower admissions standards, together with less instruction and the need for schools to keep and even graduate students regardless of their academic performance, has led to an overall decline in standards.

All of this does not bode well for our nation's future. After decades of this mentality, our children are generally more illiterate and under-informed than ever. Critical thinking and an ingrained work ethic are casualties that mean graduates aren't in a position to make intelligent choices about how to get ahead in life or make informed choices about who should lead our cities, states, and nation. The results are beginning to show up in many cities in the US, and the momentum will be difficult to reverse given much of our population's weak academic foundation.

CHAPTER 51

PHYSICAL SAFETY IS THE CORNERSTONE OF A HEALTHY SOCIETY

Politics has always been a heated forum for debating and prioritizing a society's issues. Over the years, I've seen that debate cover a broad spectrum of issues, but none are important at all in a society that doesn't adequately provide for personal safety. That has not been the case recently in a large part of the US, as personal safety and property rights have taken a backseat to other priorities. The consequences have been dire in cities where this has happened. I am sure that without the rule of law firmly in place, further erosion of these fundamental rights and needs will further degrade the quality of life.

The number-one rule for money management is to avoid losing money. In my role as a professional real estate investor, where I am responsible for investing the hard-earned savings of others and protecting that capital from loss, I've been keenly aware of the massive costs to cities that have de-prioritized physical safety and law and order and have had to avoid investing there. With the flight from these cities high and growing, there is simply too much risk associated with a poor economic future and declining real estate values. Unfortunately, the simple decision by investors like me to avoid these markets will have a self-fulfilling-prophecy effect, as the deprivation of capital will drive valuations and economic vitality lower and accelerate the desire for people to leave for greener pastures.

Incredibly, until recently, many of these locales have been among the nation's most beautiful. Suffering from wrongheaded thinking and ideology, they have become shadows of their former selves, plagued by crime and indecency. This lawlessness, coupled with a seeming lack of awareness or care on the part of leadership, repels kind and decent people and discourages investments in businesses, tourism, home buying, or any form of investment. That leads to a death spiral characterized by reduced tax revenues, negatively affecting everything from education to law enforcement.

Standing in stark contrast to these failing American cities is the recent example of El Salvador. Under the leadership of President Nabele Buekele, this country's strong stance against crime has transformed it from a global homicide capital to a country where people freely and safely live in peace. In America, the states that have embraced safety and policing of crime have benefited from an enormous influx of high-earning, productive families, whose presence will continue to energize these destinations with greater vibrancy and more opportunities. However, those states that have de-prioritized safety have seen a heavy net negative migration that will surely lead to a long downward spiraling of quality of life there.

I believe that one of the great tragedies in the US has been the inattentiveness to politics by productive citizens who are too busy working and raising children to afford to invest much time in politics. Most have always assumed that a democratic system would provide the needed checks and balances to keep the train on the rails while they went about their lives. Today, we can see clearly that this assumption has been wrong, at least in many locales, and that it is high time for each citizen to express themselves politically rather than continue to leave the political debate and the direction of our nation to a minority, fringe group who have more time on their hands to make their voices better heard. Voting and supporting law-and-order candidates who understand that without safety no other quality-of-life issue matters would seem to be a needed step to reversing things.

CHAPTER 52

THE HUNGER FOR SECURITY

I've observed that the driver of most people's actions is fear. Deep down, we fundamentally know how weak and trivial we are, powerless and doomed to suffer often until we finally die. As such, we crave any form of security, and we continually grasp at any illusions of it. This manifests itself in literally every single facet of life. People choose friends and spouses driven by this craving for security. People hold onto jobs that they hate because of this. In the world of finance where I come from, investment decisions are also often driven by the craving for security.

In the end, virtually no decisions that have been made because of our fear and desire for security can work out well. The reason for this is that the world is uncertain by nature and offers no real security. Simply seeking it puts us in direct odds with this inherent nature, which sets us up for failure. Finding comfort in the absence of security and maybe even learning to enjoy the many surprises that life has in store for you would produce far greater joy and greatly reduced disappointments and frustrations.

Many often remain in bad situations because it requires courage to walk away, as the fear of the unknown looms large and self-doubt continually whispers to us that we may not deserve anything better. My daughter Julianna decided to transfer college and leave their swim team in the middle of her freshmen year once she realized that the situation that she found herself in was unlikely to help her fulfill her potential. I've rarely been prouder of her for this display of courage. Although it was scary given that she left without a new school or team committed to her, and thus no safety net, this bold move early in her life will surely set her up to make the right choices going forward, especially the difficult ones. (Julianna did find her happy spot at SMU.)

Because of the craving for security that seems endemic to human nature, we are frequently misled by those who crave power, whether in politics, business, or personal relationships. Those people aim to seduce us by promising security in exchange for freedom. History is filled with stories of how the craving for security has caused people to trade away their freedom, follow orders, abandon their barometer of right and wrong, and do terrible things to their fellow human beings.

When pondering choices, remember that security is an illusion. There is no real job security, no unconditional permanence to any relationship, and no guarantee of safety, health, or wellness. Accepting and embracing insecurity is the key to leading an enjoyable life. On a societal level, we would also be far less likely to fall prey to would-be totalitarian leaders who aim to capitalize on our misguided quest for security by promising us a bunch of things they cannot really deliver.

CHAPTER 53

INTEGRATED SYSTEMS AND INTERSECTIONS

Compartmentalization is one of today's greatest miscalculations. In the real world, where all systems interact, there is no way to make judgments or to reach decisions by isolating and analyzing one variable without contemplating other elements of life that such a choice will naturally affect. Indeed, the most interesting and valuable contributions can often be made when working at the intersection of multiple disciplines.

Perhaps the most glaring example of this that I see is in politics. To me, a political leader must be a great businessperson. Citizens invest their hard-earned money in the form of taxes, hoping to get a well-functioning society in return. To a large extent, politics is a money management job. The politician must be able to budget, analyze competing options, and create, inspire, and manage large teams of people with appropriate checks and balances. Just as important is a required understanding of how to invest and allocate tax dollars to ensure that a desired return is achieved. Separating business from politics makes zero sense, yet we rarely consider business acumen when choosing leaders.

Consider the example of today's hunger for converting society to mostly using alternative energy rather than fossil fuels. It is clearly better if the world could find a way to pollute less and create a cleaner and healthier world, and it is unimaginable that a single human being would feel otherwise. Yet, when considering the move to cleaner energy, which is a decision that mostly considers the interests of future generations, leaders must also weigh the economic impact on those who are living today. For example, if closing coal mines *could* benefit human life two or three generations from now but *would* cause millions of jobs to be lost and those families to become dependent on governmental aid with all that would imply for their lives, what is the right decision? The point of this hypothetical is not to diminish the importance of being environmentally sensitive. It is simply to point out that there are rarely any free lunches and that math, science, business acumen, and thoughtfulness all come into play in arriving at the best decisions.

Education is also where a highly bifurcated approach is commonly taken. Knowledge is generally taught in isolation rather than in an integrated way. This approach defies the reality in which things happen. As an example, it is impossible to understand finance and economics without understanding government, just as mastering any of that while ignoring the topic of the psychology of human behavior is truly senseless. And understanding any of that without understanding people's religious or foundational belief systems, which drive how they think, react, and behave, is highly unlikely.

The same importance of intersections applies in all the world's biological, natural, and societal systems. How can they be understood in isolation or without considering the continual effects that they have on each other? For example, how can deep sea oil drilling be disconnected from a knowledge of marine biology?

Understanding integrations and interactions may very well be more important than having a deep and singular understanding of the topics themselves. I've worked at the intersection of real estate and finance and have also leaned on my insights into understanding human behavior for any success that I've achieved. I believe that these intersections where multiple skills and knowledge bases are required to thrive are where differentiation and breakthrough innovation are most likely to occur. Technology is poised to remake most fields, and those who find success will likely manage the intersection of technology and the fields themselves for the greatest success. Find intersections where you can bring together mastery in multiple subjects, and you'll find where the magic is most likely to happen.

CHAPTER 54

EARTH IS A GIANT, CHALLENGING, AND DIVERSE SCHOOL

As far as I can tell, life on earth is akin to a school, and we're all on different levels and here to learn different lessons. We operate on diverse levels of consciousness, with concurrently different sets of abilities and orientations toward understanding, interpreting, and achieving. As a result, we're destined to experience life uniquely. Yet, we tend to lump people together and judge others through our lenses by applying our standards to them. Except for demanding basic civility, which is not always a given, I believe this inclination to judge and expect mostly leads to unmet expectations, friction, and disappointment.

Despite my love for and dedication to basketball in my youth, my physical limitations ensured that my future was predestined to be different from that of my good friend Julius Erving. Julius's life would be marked by the experiences and lessons of his great basketball career, which would differ from me or from anyone else.

Some of us are born into challenging circumstances where a decent education and parental love are unavailable or in short supply. Others are born to scholarly parents who greatly emphasize knowledge and education. Some are born in rural settings where Nature is prevalent, and others are born and raised in big cities, wholly disconnected from Nature. Despite our deep differences, we must find ways to coexist in this world. Yet we must also understand that friction is inherent. The goals of some will naturally be different and may conflict directly with those of others.

I also believe we have a misguided notion that our world is something to be "saved." That does not seem to be the game plan here. Instead, it is a world that provides interesting opportunities to learn and grow. Although it is tempting to imagine that we all see things roughly the same since we look pretty much alike, it is essential to remember that we're not the same. The Bible is an excellent place to learn from because it has chronicled history and has influenced so much thinking while teaching its readers through timeless stories. Few are as straightforward as Cain and Abel, earth's first siblings, wherein Cain, the hunter, killed his younger brother, the softer one, in a jealous rage.

People, even brothers, are all on different levels of consciousness, which means that some will be hunters just looking to conquer and kill, and others are looking for peace and friendship. Things can be challenging when these two types meet, as they do daily. The amazing thing is that in a world with so much diversity, if we can maintain civility and be empathetic, there is so much that we can learn just by sharing with each other.

CHAPTER 55

GOVERNMENT IS
INHERENTLY DANGEROUS

My thinking has evolved from being a true libertarian to acknowledging that government does have value, which I see as being mostly based on preventing society from slipping into a state of anarchy and violence. Except for staying on top of that specific risk, I find that the federal government has little value. I retain a healthy fear of its power, and thus I advocate for the smallest federal government possible. In my mind, a large and powerful federal government introduces the kind of totalitarian risks that have been seen in societies gone wrong such as Nazi Germany and the Soviet Union, and that have been so well chronicled by futurist authors such as George Orwell.

When thinking about government, it is important to distinguish between local and federal. Government is most efficient and accountable when its powers are local rather than federal. Local government is in a far better position to produce value given their proximity to their constituents and their resulting ability to be empathetic and responsive to citizens' needs. Also, that proximity and the fact that these politicians come from the communities that they oversee is a major contributing factor to local government efficacy and accountability.

I know of so many people who react to my fears of big federal government by pointing to big business as a culprit of many things wrong, and who feel more comfortable trusting government power than business power. Although I am quick to admit that the private sector and big business are far from perfect, that thinking is rooted in highly flawed logic. The business world, by its nature, is a competitive arena where success and the resulting power flow to enterprises that bring value to consumers. In that world, there is plenty of competition. When a company stumbles and fails to satisfy its customers, there are many others ready to push them aside, and no one is there to prop them up. In my lifetime, major and dominant companies such as Palm, BlackBerry, Countrywide, Lehman Brothers, and Bear Stearns have all failed and disappeared and many others, such as IBM and Xerox, have waned in prominence.

In stark contrast to this competitive business landscape, which provides genuine checks to power and where success is generally dependent upon the ability to produce value, the federal government has no such competition. It operates as a monopoly – with massive, unchecked powers that allow it to remain in power for long periods despite having very few satisfied customers. It makes the laws (many of which it exempts itself from) and then uses the courts, guns, and prisons to enforce them.

Unlike the business world, which has been rife with turnover in my life, Congress has seen little change despite approval levels that have always been exceptionally low. In fact, some individual Congresspeople have been in office for much of my adult life despite very spotty records of achievement.

Our public education system is another prominent example of the shortcomings of government control and the attendant absence of checks and balances that would naturally come from competition. It has been an unmitigated disaster, yet it remains intact, punishing us all with its incompetence. Despite this history of failure, any efforts to introduce change, such as charter schools, have been thwarted by the unchecked power of government protecting teachers' unions in return for votes.

A society that facilitates greatness and provides for broader opportunities for its citizens to express their best selves is likely to be a society that has a greater reliance on the private sector for its economic vibrancy and benefits from a light-touch federal government.

CHAPTER 56

EQUALITY IS NOT THE POINT

Inequality begins at birth and cannot be fixed. Some people are born prettier, smarter, or stronger than others. No one is born with the same mix of attributes and circumstances. The fact that inequality begins at birth is a strong indicator that equality is not the design of human life.

However, fortunately, birth advantages are not always good predictors of future success. The best athlete in high school, who may have parlayed his or her early physical advantage into social popularity and more, often finds that similar success in adulthood is not guaranteed. Similarly, straight A students who may have benefited from greater parental focus and attention are not always the ones who launch companies or make the largest impacts in adulthood.

No one can argue when a society strives to provide for relatively equal opportunities with a concurrent high degree of social mobility that inspires people to do their best. However, when politicians promise to create equality of outcomes, it's instructive to recall that equality is not something that can be mandated. In fact, the idea of mandating equality of outcomes is antithetical to society's best interests. It suppresses any inclination to work hard and deprives us of the magical

145

things produced by people who are inspired to great efforts by the promise of outsized rewards. We must run quickly from aspiring despots who use the false promise of equality as a tool to gain power over us. The litany of carnage and sadness left in the wake of people like Joseph Stalin, Chairman Mao, Hugo Chavez of Venezuela, and Fidel Castro in Cuba is a history of 100% failure.

More benign political actors have also done real damage through the misguided pursuit of equality. Over the past several decades in the US, well-meaning politicians observed that a college education generally pointed to a better career potential and earnings stream. Armed with this observation, they encouraged more youth to pursue college degrees and then facilitated access by expanding government student loan programs. In fact, in the two-plus decades since the 1990s, the percentage of high school students going directly to college has jumped by 73%.

Prior to this government-induced shift, when fewer students entered the workforce with a college degree their degrees commanded respect and a better career. As more graduates hit the workforce with their college degrees, the degree itself lost value. This is a simple supply /demand economic reality that should have been obvious decades ago before so many lives were misdirected and became buried in college loans that yielded career opportunities that are less than what was hoped for. Because this happened while technology proliferated with a targeted aim of reducing labor costs by cutting jobs, the societal costs associated with this blunder have only compounded. This mistaken effort by government also helps to explain the student loan problem and a college graduate population serving coffee at Starbucks or working other similar jobs that were clearly not their aim at graduation.

We must live in a manner that is consistent with the construct of the world. Inequality is a force that must be reckoned with and accepted. It can't be mandated away. The good news is that as long as we have freedom, we can all work hard to make something pretty darn good of ourselves, regardless of our initial station in life.

CHAPTER 57

GOVERNMENT IS A COMPANY AND TAXPAYERS ARE THE INVESTORS

I believe that there is huge misunderstanding regarding taxes. Those advocating for lower taxes are frequently caricatured as being greedy and selfish. A common refrain we hear from tax-loving politicians who want more money and power coursing through their control is that these people refuse to "pay their fair share." Nobody is quite sure what that amount is, and the accusations continue even though, as of this writing, the top 25% of income producers pay about 89% of all US federal income taxes, reflective of a highly progressive system.

I look at taxes as an investment of capital into a political management team, expecting that they execute a strategy to produce a healthy and functional society. Everyone wants to live in the best possible society characterized by safe streets, great education and health care for all, affordable living expenses, and fulfilled lives. Citizens would happily invest through taxation to support such a society that they and their children would enjoy.

Unfortunately, the US doesn't produce such a society for its citizens and hasn't for a long time. For example, no country spends more per capita than the United States on things like public education and health care, yet we're saddled with horrible results. Given this pathetic record that our politicians have of producing very poor value in the form of a dysfunctional society, it should not be surprising that people would try to minimize their tax bill. In such a situation, who can be faulted for wanting to minimize their investment exposure into this losing management team and their failed strategies?

With a better management team in place producing consistently strong results in the form of a vibrant society, I have no doubt that most citizens would need little coercion to dig into their savings to support such a system. In today's reality, with a government producing poor value, who would want to willingly invest their hard-earned money?

CHAPTER 58

THE PERSUASION INDUSTRY

Have you ever wondered why so much money is spent by corporations on marketing and advertising? Or why politicians are constantly busy raising money so that they can run a successful campaign? What do you suppose they need all that money for? If the products being touted were desirable, or the politicians were worthy and qualified, then would we really need much to be persuaded to become advocates for them? Wouldn't we naturally gravitate their way without the need for too much other than alerting us to their basic and obvious merits?

The reality is that tremendous efforts and resources are being invested daily to manipulate us all to take actions and to make choices that may be antithetical to our best interests, and that we probably would not choose if we weren't brainwashed. There are thousands of highly educated people who spend their lives manipulating us to buy things that we never knew we wanted, don't need, and probably wouldn't want if we properly understood the consequences. That is so sad and screwed up on every level.

We blithely go about our lives, idiotically acquiescing to being manipulated and suffering the horrible consequences – whether it be that we get too fat eating junk or that we see our society in decline because we choose the wrong leaders. If the world is going to change for the better, we must become far more aware and demanding as a society.

I have an affection and admiration for the rationale of the traditional capitalist model and human freedom. However, I see much of the marketing and advertising industries, which some refer to as *the persuasion industry,* as predators that prey on our inherent weaknesses for financial gain. To understand about how we arrived at the modern American-style consumer-driven economic model it would be instructive to read *An Affluent Society*, published by Harvard economist John Kenneth Galbraith in 1958. In it, you'll learn that the modern system of advertising and marketing first appeared in the 1950s in response to the then-newfound belief that boosting GDP was the be-all and end-all goal of a healthy society. The actionable goal was to influence citizens to spend more money. Fast-forwarding to today, this system has influenced us all to borrow too much money to buy things that we can't afford and frequently would not even want if we gave it some thought. It is a system that has preyed on people's competitive inclinations and has manipulated us through envy. It would not be a stretch to suggest that this system and the actions it has inspired can be directly tied to many of the major problems that we now face in the world. Most notably, it has created an insane level of indebtedness that acts as a huge burden on our society and inhibits growth and opportunities for fulfillment and happiness.

There are two plausible outcomes for this misguided behavior. Our society can experience a painful crash; then, faced with existential failure, we can reflect on what brought us there to learn and grow. Or we can elevate ourselves to a higher level of observation and awareness, change our behavior, and spare ourselves the crash. It's not clear which will happen, and history seems to indicate that the more painful journey is more common, but either way, we'll learn an important lesson and hopefully grow from it.

CHAPTER 59

THE WORLD IS SELF-CORRECTING

In economics, the concept of recurring cycles is broadly accepted. It is based on the notion that humans react in a herd-like manner. These cycles begin when prosperity creates a broad complacency about risk, which naturally leads to excesses in spending, borrowing, investing, and ultimately in prices paid for all things. Inevitably cracks begin to appear. Typically, companies or people who borrowed too much and/or expanded too quickly end up failing. These early failures make the rest of us nervous as we consider that we also may have borrowed and bought too much and probably paid prices that were too high. This nervousness leads us to begin to sell assets and to curtail further spending, thus creating both a market and an economic downturn. Downturns ultimately lead to lower prices for labor and goods, as demand for both wanes. In turn, those low prices inspire opportunists to begin to buy and expand their businesses, which stimulates prices to begin to move higher, making those early buys appear to have been prescient. These successes then inspire others to become optimistic, leading to a new resurgence and the beginning of the next cycle.

Another simple way to see this natural cycle is through the self-correcting nature of prices. When the demand for something begins to strain its supply, prices for that something naturally rise. Ultimately, prices will rise to levels that will inspire more production, yet simultaneously repel demand. This combination of too many goods having been produced relative to the demand for them will naturally lead to price reductions, as sellers try to induce buyers to take their larger inventories. There is no need for any intervention by government or any other external force in order to correct markets. Markets and economies, like much of the other world systems, are naturally self-correcting.

Economic cyclicality is a prime example of the world's self-correcting nature, but there are many others. In 2016, America elected Donald Trump, an impolitic man who prided himself as a no-nonsense doer who ran on the patriotic premise of American exceptionalism, using the slogan "Make America Great Again." He followed eight years of Barack Obama, who was erudite, highly diplomatic, and an unabashed globalist who invented the concept of America "leading from behind." After four years with Trump's chaotic style, America swung to Joe Biden, its oldest president ever and a man who promised calm, the antithesis of Donald Trump.

In the end, we probably should not get too excited about things going our way or too despondent when they don't. Things are always bound to change and self-correct.

CHAPTER 60

TEACHING PEOPLE TO FISH

"Give a man a fish, and you feed him for a day; teach a man to fish, and you feed him for a lifetime." This insight is quite old, yet it is constantly forgotten, ignored, and unappreciated by large segments of our society. The merits are so straightforward and obvious that they should not require many words to explain. My ancestors understood well how important education is in giving us the foundation of capabilities that we need to achieve, produce, not burden others, and ultimately gain true self-esteem.

Politicians and others throughout history, disturbed by poverty or the unequal distribution of resources, have frequently ignored this lesson and have attempted to redistribute wealth. They have taken "fish" from some who have an abundance and handed it to others who are needier. Interestingly, although no effort of this type has ever succeeded, the siren song of receiving free things, and the ability of those seeking power to manipulate by offering these free things, has perpetuated this disastrous approach.

The failure of redistribution is rooted in two simple facts. First, once pursued, society will devalue productivity in favor of adopting and rewarding a taker mentality. By doing this, the total pool of resources ultimately shrinks away. Second, the government, wielding massive power in its role as the arbiter of resource distribution, naturally becomes corrupt over time, siphoning off too much of society's resources for itself while producing nothing. Today, Venezuela is a great example of an incredibly wealthy nation with a proud history that has been devastated by this flawed ideology.

Although there is a continual debate as to which societal construct is superior, I firmly believe that the best is the one that inspires people to excel rather than one that depresses their initiative or their individuality. It is one that rewards action, creativity, and productivity. It is one that inspires us to dream because we can believe that even our most ambitious goals are possible. It is one that encourages personal responsibility and respect for others. A healthy society provides its people with a great education that enables them to fulfill their highest productive potential, leading them to joy and higher self-esteem that can only come from this type of accomplishment. Greatness comes from striving, learning, and ultimately producing value. A redistributionist society is antithetical to greatness, and it is no surprise that societies that have pursued this path have seen their producers and aspiring producers flee for other places.

It is difficult for me to understand any other position. As I see it, we are given a life to live. Top-down solutions that inhibit or deprive us of the joy of the journey and the fulfillment of meeting challenges are the opposite of what works. A society should empower its people to find its purpose and to learn while continually growing and striving to meet our challenges.

CHAPTER 61

THE TREADMILL OF LIFE IS MOVING TOO FAST

We are all on a proverbial treadmill that we cannot get off, nor should we really waste any time trying. The world has resources that we all require to survive, and we must go out and produce something of value so that we can earn our share of them. This is the treadmill at work. This is our reality, and rather than condemn it or fight it, we should simply acknowledge it and understand that it is a part of the human experience and the formula of purpose.

I have noticed that the speed of the treadmill has continued to increase massively during my lifetime and is now operating at dangerously high levels, undermining the quality of life for us all. The signs of this are all around. In the time of my childhood, it was rare for women to work. And although it is true that opportunities for women to work were not as abundant back in the 1960s and prior, it is also true and often overlooked that until recently women didn't need to work for a family's financial security. The two-worker household was rare in my childhood when women could choose to be full-time mothers and leaders of the home, and families were the beneficiaries of the women's time and skills in this critically important job. I have two daughters who are extremely smart and have incredible potential, and I am thrilled that they live at a time when women are free to pursue whatever their career dreams may be. However, a woman should also find pride in choosing to be a full-time mom and leader of the home, as this can also be a legitimate dream. Today, most women will not have this choice because the treadmill is flying, and their income is required.

Another sign of the treadmill's speed is the amount of increased road traffic. Earlier in my career, roads were mostly clear, and traffic moved smoothly even during rush hour. Today it is common for the rush-hour crush to begin as early as 5:00 a.m. with four-hour blocks of stop-and-go traffic in the morning and evening commutes.

The quality of medical care that we now receive is another indicator. As a child, when I got sick, my mom would have the family doctor over for a house call. He would care for me in the comfort of my room and then also find the time to sit for tea or coffee and chat with my folks. Now, we dread going to the doctor's office. The wait is interminable, and the doctor typically has several people sitting in different examination rooms and a packed waiting room that they bounce between while trying to balance an outsized patient load with decent quality of care.

The speedier treadmill has many other far-reaching negative consequences, including producing an overly stressed population hooked on anti-depressants, generations of youth robbed of the love and education that only parental time and attention can provide, and an unhealthy level of competitiveness for material things that has created an envy-ridden society. Why no one examines this more carefully is one of the great travesties of modern society. Politicians love to promise growth but seem to mostly ignore quality of life as the more important goal.

CHAPTER 62

THE TRUTH ABOUT MONEY AND FINANCE

Most people have an unhealthy relationship with money. Those same people often say money is the embodiment of evil. How ridiculous and off base! The truth is that money simply facilitates the exchange of value with others.

For example, if I raise chickens that produce eggs, I must exchange those eggs to fulfill my family's other needs. Nobody can subsist on only eggs alone, right? Maybe my family wants a car, but the car dealer would never exchange a car for tons of eggs. He doesn't need all those eggs nor wants to be in the egg business. He only wants to be in the car business. Money is the facilitator that lets me sell my eggs to those who want them, allowing me to save money that I can use to buy a car. It is the common denominator and a tool that creates the valuable function of commerce on which all of society is built.

Finance is the system that enables money to move fluidly through a society, ideally from savers with excess funds that can be transferred to and invested with those who need that money. That is the core function of banks, investment firms, stock exchanges, and other similar institutions. Finance facilitates transactions between those who need the capital for productive efforts by rewarding savers with a return in the forms of profits or an interest rate for investing their money with those who will use that money for productive agendas. This return is the proper reward for the risk involved in possibly losing some of that money in a bad investment or not having access to the money for some time. That forsaken access to capital is often an unnoticed aspect of the trade-off of making an investment. During the time that the investment is outstanding, the investor loses access to the money, which means that other investment opportunities cannot be pursued or that the joys associated with consumption, such as buying things or taking vacations, may have to be put off.

To make this all clearer, imagine that I lend you $100,000 for you to begin a business. There is a risk that your business will fail, and you won't be able to repay me the $100,000. There is also the possibility that you will succeed and that your business might be worth much more than the $100,000. For taking this risk, I would naturally be entitled to share in the successful outcome if that occurs. That is why a return on my investment would be justified. Also, while you have my $100,000, I can't invest it into other opportunities that may come along and could be even more promising than investing in your company. I also can't use that $100,000 it to take my family on a family vacation or to buy a new car. In return for giving up access to my $100,000 until you've returned it to me, I would naturally be entitled to earn a return on that money.

In a society where this system of money and finance functions properly, growth and prosperity are far more likely. This system is a crucial pillar in creating the possibility of social mobility, as savers seeking a return on their capital will naturally direct their investment capital toward those with the best prospects for success. People with good ideas and a willingness to work hard will naturally attract money in a society with a healthy financial system, and some of these people will create tomorrow's companies, large and small, that will lead to employment opportunities for many people.

Money and finance are sometimes blamed for human greed and other dark human qualities. That is analogous to blaming food for gluttony. It makes no sense. Money and finance are tools of a healthy capitalist system that facilitate a prosperous society.

Another point regarding the system of money and finance has to do with inherent fairness. Everyone wants to receive more in exchange for their time or products, whether it is a company seeking to maximize profits or an employee seeking to maximize pay. For example, no prospective employee shows up at work and says, "I know you're offering a salary of $100,000 per year, but I'd prefer if you paid me $75,000." So, when a company is hiring for a job, the desire to maximize productivity and profits will lead that company to hire the individual who will best contribute to the company's success. In this type of system, no preference would be given based on any other variable besides merit.

Pure capitalism is blind to skin color, nationality, race, religion, sexual orientation, political belief, or any variable other than competence. It is inherently the only fair system, requiring no intervening outside hands because it is self-policing. Companies that favor other variables instead of competence and productivity will lose market share and ultimately be driven out of business by those companies that only consider competence when choosing people to employ or partner with.

CHAPTER 63

CAPITALISM . . .

Capitalism is a system that creates incentives in the form of material rewards in exchange for producing value for society. Think of it as a system that communicates society's desires in the form of pay. When we see someone making a ton of money in a capitalist society, we can infer that this individual is investing their time in a way that is producing something that society wants. When we see someone struggling and making little money, we can infer that this individual is not producing something that society wants very much, or is producing something that is already broadly and abundantly available. The reward system reflects society's wants at that time. So, a great drug dealer or athlete being highly paid is simply a reflection of society's priorities at that moment. For better or worse, these people are producing something that our society prizes highly.

Capitalism is not always pretty, just as looking in the mirror is not at times. Capitalism is also not gentle. But it does provide honest and natural feedback that pushes us away from endeavors we may not be well suited for or that we may love to do but whose output is not highly desired or needed and thus pays poorly. It moves us toward discovering a path that will position us to produce our maximum value for society, as measured by what the reward is for success down that path. This push can feel unpleasant in many ways. We may dream to be a stage actor or a singer, but we may not have the skill. We may love gardening or teaching elementary school, but the pay for these pursuits wouldn't provide us with the financial security that we crave for our family.

Capitalism works best when people optimize their productive energies for society's benefit, as measured by society's desires at that time. With honest and healthy competition in place, capitalism inspires everyone to produce their best efforts. Capitalism pushes us to be our best and overcome the human attraction to inertia while simultaneously finding self-worth from a noble pursuit of excellence and contribution. By inspiring this societal effort toward productivity, capitalism also leads to the advancement of society and creates more opportunities for the most people possible.

Some people are frustrated by capitalism and develop a natural antipathy toward it. Many are just not good at the game of capitalism. They can't identify skills they possess that would produce value for others and that would be highly rewarded. Or, they may have skills that are broadly available and thus not highly prized. Others are committed to pursuing their passions without regard to financial reward. All of these people are voices of moderation in a healthy political debate on how a society should be structured. They will remind us that maybe a society that rewards drug dealers and athletes as it does while not rewarding teachers very well may need to think about how to rebalance its priorities.

CHAPTER 64

. . . NOT CRONYISM

Many people abhor capitalism for the wrong reasons. What they really hate is cronyism, and they've mistaken it for capitalism. Cronyism is cheating, plain and simple. It is grotesque and unfair. And it has the complete opposite effect on society that capitalism does. Cronyism deflates effort rather than inspires it and depresses a society rather than uplifts it.

Cronyism involves the manipulative and powerful hand of government intruding on the naturally merit-based capitalist system in a way that influences outcomes in favor of those who are "friends" of those in powerful government positions. It is among the most destructive forces that any society faces and emanates completely from increased governmental power, not from the private sector. A nation with a strong private sector and a smaller, less intrusive government will suffer far less from the disastrous effects of cronyism.

Cronyists are clever and especially adept at hiding and misdirecting people's inherent hatred of their unfair and destructive ways by blaming the private sector and free market capitalism. They plant the seeds in people's minds that capitalism is to blame for these distortions and unfair outcomes. You'll often hear them blaming all ills on "big business," hoping that you won't notice how they've tipped the scales in the favor of select businesses that they favor, and probably have some corrupt relationship with. These cronyists will advocate that capitalism must be heavily managed by the government to ensure that people get a fair deal. This deceitful practice of government bureaucrats and their partners misdirecting blame and grabbing even more manipulative control has worked too often throughout history and will probably be with us until the end of time.

The best we can hope for is to choose to be more active politically and make wise choices as to whom we elect to govern us. In this process, it is worthwhile to pay careful attention to a candidate's past, demonstrated moral character, work experiences, and established skill set. Falling for those who crave power, whatever their other appeal, is likely to result in a period of heightened cronyism.

CHAPTER 65

THE LIMITATIONS OF CAPITALISM

Although I am generally an admirer of the inspirational forces of capitalism, which can lead us to live purposeful lives and create a society that is continuously improving, I am not blind to its limitations.

One of these limitations is how capitalism does not discriminate between rewarding those who produce real value and those who prey on human weaknesses to generate wealth for themselves. Another shortcoming worth noting is that capitalism does not properly differentiate between those who succeed by creating jobs and opportunities for others and those who succeed by destroying them and limiting opportunities for others.

Pablo Escobar, the notorious Colombian drug dealer, was richly rewarded for creating a massive business that processed and distributed illegal drugs. There is no disputing that Escobar was an accomplished capitalist. Like other mega-successful business leaders, he understood human nature well and he created and led a massive business that was hugely profitable. Escobar identified a large, unmet demand and filled it. The problem is that his business destroyed millions of lives and the demand that he identified, cultivated, and then met was driven by human weakness and addiction. That he reaped the rewards he did was clearly antithetical to society's best interests.

You can argue that justice was ultimately served for many people in Escobar's network with death or long prison sentences. That may be true, but because he and others in the drug trade reaped massive financial rewards, many have been encouraged to follow in his footsteps, which perpetuates that predatorial business.

The illegal drug business is only one, albeit an extreme example of industries that reward those who prey on human weakness and addiction. How about the sugar industry, gaming industry, and social media business models that are built on taking advantage of the brain's addictive nature? Like drugs, these businesses create massive financial rewards by feeding human weakness and addiction, and generally without the risk of incarceration. Should the success of an executive or innovator in those businesses be rewarded similarly to one in other industries? I'd suggest that in a healthy society, the answer would be a resounding no.

And what about the impact of technology-based businesses? Most examples of wealth created during the Industrial Revolution can also be tied to great societal benefits, including consequential job creation. Henry Ford was not broadly thought of as a terrific guy, but his innovation and hard work uplifted many lives by creating significant opportunities for others. In that light, the wealth that he was rewarded with was justified and logical. In stark contrast to Ford and others like him from that period, the titans of the technology era are mostly reaping massive financial rewards for destroying jobs. They have unmercifully outsourced jobs to other nations where human rights are questionable and cheap labor plentiful or simply eliminated the need for human labor through automation. In fact, the main promise of most tech companies is improved efficiency, which is really a nice way of saying "reduced human labor cost." In this era, we must rightly question if that same capitalist system that inspired and rewarded Ford and others like him is working properly for the best interest of our society today. Like all systems that have been in place for a long time, capitalism probably needs to be reinvented to best serve today's world.

CHAPTER 66

CANARIES IN THE COAL MINE

The "canary in a coal mine" metaphor originates from a time when miners would take canaries underground with them to see if deadly gases were present. If so, the canaries would die first, giving the miners an early warning that they should get out immediately. Similarly, I've noticed that the people operating on the fringes of society in possession of unusual and unconventional ideas can be useful "canaries" for society.

Their words often make no sense to us, and they seem either crazy or ignorant, or both. However, when their collective voices grow loud enough to be heard, that is often a sign of something disquieting that ought to be addressed before it grows and gets out of hand. Today's appeal of extremism on the one hand and socialism on the other among factions of America's youth, and their willingness to support dubious leaders, is one such example. It shouldn't be dismissed as pure folly but instead requires serious thought and examination inasmuch as it reveals trouble brewing just below the surface that can easily gain traction if ignored.

Such loud voices, especially from younger generations, should prompt us all to question how well the pillars of our society are functioning. So many of these foundations were built for a different era, some going back to the time of the horse and buggy. It would be unwise to imagine that everything that worked in past times would also be relevant, let alone optimal, in today's different and rapidly changing tech-dominated time. The canaries are chirping. We should all be listening.

CHAPTER 67

CLASS ENVY IS A DANGEROUS POISON

I grew up poor. We had nothing. Literally no savings whatsoever. I attended college with financial aid and loans and worked full-time throughout. In fact, I've been working since about age nine. I knew that if I didn't find work after college, I wouldn't be able to eat. In my career, I achieved great heights, made good money, and found my way into a completely different socioeconomic peer group than the one I grew up with. This unique path that I've walked has afforded me many insights and enabled a special level of empathy that I feel is a great blessing.

One thing I've learned is that poor and rich can rarely be friends. Of course, there are exceptions. One of these is when money is unimportant to one or both, which is quite rare and generally the privilege of a higher state of awareness than most people have. Another is when the poorer person remains ambitious and is pursuing dreams of producing value in the world. In that situation, inspiration replaces envy when the ambitious person takes pride and joy in his or her pursuit of dreams.

I first noticed socioeconomic class distinction as a child, and I found it to be repugnant. As I got older and had more real-world experience, I began to see that although it is sad and possibly offensive, it is also understandable. The world has resources that people compete for to live well. In this competition, those who have specific skills and learn how to successfully employ them are rewarded with greater portions of these resources. Because of this, rich and poor people being near each other can be akin to the sound of nails on a chalkboard – a constant reminder of the inherent unfairness of life itself.

This seemingly unfair resource allocation seems to be how human life is set up. The Indian culture has long handled this by operating a strict caste system that precludes social mixing between classes. Other governments have long attempted to legislate inequality away, and every effort has failed miserably. Ironically, these efforts have often fueled greater class envy and rage. This envy will continue to cause human pain without a broader increase in awareness that leads us to embrace a less materialistic focus.

I believe that a healthy society will have a system that efficiently redistributes enough resources to ensure that everyone lives a decent life that provides for basic needs while at the same time allowing for outsized rewards to flow to those who make outsized contributions.

CHAPTER 68

THE BASIS OF CYNICISM: THE MILGRAM STUDY

In the aftermath of the Holocaust, a Yale University psychologist named Stanley Milgram was perplexed at the thought of normal Germans participating in mass murder. He decided to conduct a study to test people's inclinations to be obedient and to follow directives from authority figures.

The experiment involved separating test subjects into pairs composed of a teacher and a student. The students were told to study and memorize word pairings, which they'd be tested on. Then each teacher was placed one at a time inside of a room facing a wall of levers with signage at each lever indicating an electrical voltage level that ran all the way up to 450 volts, a dangerously high level. There was a Yale faculty member in the room, and the teacher was asked to read a word and then have the student recite from memory the corresponding word from the pairings. An incorrect answer from the student was to be punished with an increasing voltage applied by the teacher that would be sent into the student's body.

The student was ostensibly seated on the other side of a solid wall and could not be seen but was heard. Unbeknownst to the teachers, all the students were dismissed and replaced by an actor, who cried in anguish and begged for mercy as the voltage increased with each incorrect answer. When the teacher expressed reluctance at administering an ever-higher voltage for an incorrect answer, the Yale faculty member in the room would cajole him with remarks such as, "This is an important work," or "You must continue on for the study to be of any value." Amazingly, inside of a Yale University building in Hartford, Connecticut, 65% of the subjects in the role of "teacher" went all the way, following orders and delivering unimaginable levels of voltage to the people called "students" simply for getting word pairings wrong. In case you were quick to give credit to the other 35% who wouldn't go all the way to the 450-volt maximum, not a single teacher quit before the 300-volt level.

It pains me to say that this study may be the most important one ever done as to the understanding of human behavior. Every day, I need to try to overlook this study so I don't become mired in complete cynicism about humanity and the world. It is specifically the sentiments that are naturally felt when contemplating this study and balanced against many of the pro-human/pro-freedom thoughts that I've articulated in this book that cuts right to the core of the omnipresent concept of duality. Opposite beliefs can and must coexist somehow. Living well requires us to be appropriately cynical while at the same time remaining hopeful.

CHAPTER 69

A FINAL THOUGHT . . .
THE WORLD WON'T END

In 2008, it seemed to those who understood the global financial system and who appreciated how dependent human life had become on its health and survival that the world as we knew it was flirting dangerously with an end. The Federal Reserve Bank did the unthinkable – literally print trillions of dollars from thin air and inject that new money into the economy, hoping to stave off a second coming of the Great Depression. To many, this action risked rendering the dollar and all global currency meaningless. I recall vividly wondering what would happen if the average worker refused to accept this paper currency of now questionable valuable in return for his hard work that week. If that happened, and the value of the national currency was broadly doubted, I thought that it was all over and that the unthinkable was possible.

I've heard it said that society is something like five or six missed meals from complete breakdown, and I began to imagine how that would look. It was frightening. Then, in an epiphany, I realized these worst-case fears would never come to pass. I figured that as bad as things may get, no one wants the world to end. Everyone will make whatever sacrifice is required to ensure its survival. I see this as a large and inadvertent conspiracy. It is this human instinct to persist that we can take comfort in, even in the darkest moments. It is this instinct that will catalyze a resolution to virtually any existential threats and will ensure that the world won't end. This understanding is comforting on a personal level and is something that can also be quite instructive in the investment world.

I am often accused by those in my industry of being a bit too negative or pessimistic, or cynical, and I suppose that it is true. I do see very clearly the challenges of life and the dark side of human nature. But I consider myself to be quite positive and even optimistic, understanding that life is meant to be hard, but that it is so to provide us with the proper opportunities to learn and to grow. Thus, I find this thought to be a fittingly optimistic message on which to end this book. The world won't end.

I wish you all a beautiful life journey of discovery.

Ethan

ACKNOWLEDGMENTS

The process of producing this book has involved living my life and learning so much from so many people along the way. I must especially acknowledge my primary teachers – my parents, Samuel and Arlene – who set for me the example of living in an aware state, always asking, and forever seeking meaning. I appreciate deeply Bret Colson, who has been the greatest editor one can have in that he always pushed me to produce the best version of my ideas. I also want to give a large shout-out to Wiley, especially to Zachary Schisgal and Shannon Vargo, who saw a writer in me before I was one.

ABOUT THE AUTHOR

Ethan Penner grew up in the blue-collar community of Yonkers, New York. From an early age, his scholarly parents imbued him with a seeker mentality that would later become the foundation of his curiosity and confidence.

Those traits served him well early in his career when Ethan began a rise to prominence, eventually being regarded as a Wall Street pioneer who reshaped the real estate finance industry in the 1990s. He built a real estate finance operation from the ground up, redefining the industry to become the largest such firm in US history. His innovations revived and brought much-needed liquidity to a collapsed industry, helping many commercial real estate owners survive during this challenging time.

In recognition of his visionary successes, *Real Estate Finance* magazine named Ethan one of the US real estate industry's 10 most important leaders of the real estate industry in the 1990s. He was also voted the Financial Services Executive of the Year for five consecutive years and was included in the *Global Finance* magazine list of the world's most powerful people in finance. In 2011, the Real Estate Forum voted him one of the industry's 65 living legends in their 65th-anniversary issue.

Ethan approaches real estate investing from the perspective of one who studies and anticipates human behavior. His unique blend of philosophy, politics, economics, sociology, and religion heavily influence his work and his relationships. Many of those same thoughts and points of view are the basis for writing *Greatness Is a Choice*.

He remains an in-demand industry speaker and continues to author articles for several leading real estate investing and finance publications, including the *Wall Street Journal* and *Institutional Real Estate Investor*, among others. He also shares his considerable knowledge as an adjunct professor at Pepperdine University.

INDEX

empathy, 82
peace, imagining, 74
perspectives (contrast), 5
saving, notion (problem), 140
self-correction, ability, 151–152

Wozniak, Steve, 114

Xerox, prominence (decline), 142

Zedong, Mao, 146